JUSTICE & REFORM
IF PRISON WORKED

SUE WOOD

UK Book Publishing.com

Design, typesetting and publishing by UK Book Publishing

www.ukbookpublishing.com

ISBN: 978-1-917329-26-2

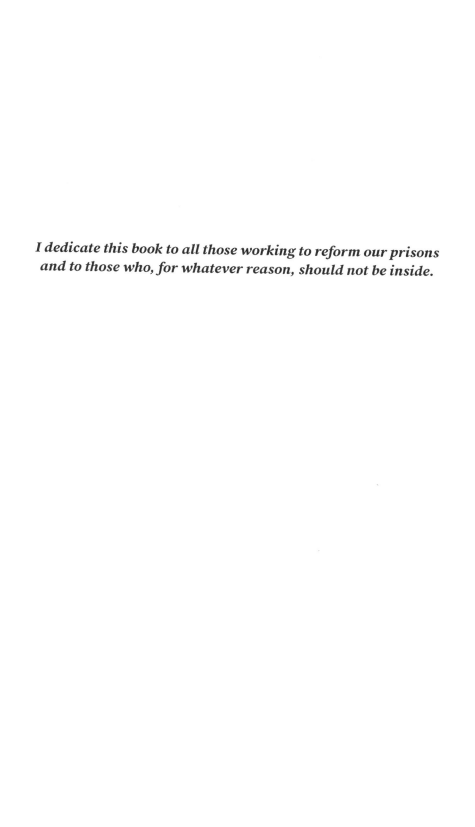

I dedicate this book to all those working to reform our prisons and to those who, for whatever reason, should not be inside.

CONTENTS

PREFACE

J ust today, Wednesday June 26th 2024, the human rights lawyer Cherie Blair, wife of the former Prime Minister Sir Tony Blair, called for fewer women to be sent to prison. She also called for the end of pregnant women being sent to jail.

Oh my word when have we ever heard that before?

Well we could start in 1813 when Elizabeth Fry visited Newgate prison. She was horrified by the conditions she saw there. The prison was full with women and children, and they were kept in overcrowded and unsanitary conditions. She wrote in a letter to one of her children about her early visits stating *"I have lately been twice to Newgate to see after the poor prisoners who had poor little infants without clothing, or with very little and I think if you saw how small a piece of bread they are each allowed a day you would be very sorry"*.

Or we could go back even further to John Howard, High Sheriff of Bedford, who having visited several hundred prisons across England, Scotland and Wales and wider Europe, then published the first edition of *The State of the Prisons* in 1777. This was not just about women and children in prison but about the whole prison estate. It included very detailed accounts of the prisons he had visited, including plans and maps, together with detailed instructions on the necessary improvements, especially regarding hygiene and cleanliness, the lack of which was causing many deaths.

Well there were other prison reformers of course but these are the two most famous ones.

The Howard Association was founded in 1866 by admirers of John Howard and The Penal Reform League was founded in 1907 and had a proud history of defending imprisoned suffragettes. Just over 100 years ago in 1921 they both came together to form the Howard League for Penal Reform under the leadership of Margery Fry who was the great niece of Elizabeth Fry. It is the oldest penal reform organisation in the world.

So with such eminent beginnings and with over 100 years of further eminent prison reformers, lawyers, politicians, prison inspectors, journalists and writers all focused on the state of our prisons, why is it that Cherie Blair feels it is necessary to make a request such as the one at the beginning of this prologue?

Surely, by now, our prisons must be well-run, efficient, purposeful and humane. And if prison is working then re-offending will be at an all-time low.

If you know anything about the modern prison system you might be able to see where we are going here. But this is not an academic thesis about the need for prison reform as there are plenty of those already. This is my personal story and I invite you to come along with me to see if we can find some answers.

YOUNG OFFENDERS

In 1991 I read that a 16 year old boy had committed suicide whilst in prison on remand. He was sent to Feltham Prison in West London, about 200 miles from his home, for 188 days. While he was there, alone, he was told that his grandmother had died. A prison officer found him sobbing in his cell, where he was confined for as much as 21 hours a day. Social services denied him permission to go to the funeral. Shortly afterwards, he was found dead, hanged from his barred window. He had been sent to Feltham for setting fire to a shed. I wrote the following poem in August 1991 for all young people who are locked up.

NOBODY'S CHILD

I warn you, don't try to push me around,
Others have done it, but I've always found
That they soon back down when I kick and I bite
When I throw things and swear and I shout and I fight.
I know I'm aggressive. I know that I'm wild
But I'll stand on my own; for I'm nobody's child.

One day they tell me, someone out there
Will want me, and love me, and tell me they care.
Meanwhile they threaten, they plead and they frown.
Now just you conform they say – just you calm down.
They have to be joking; I'm not meek and mild
I'm me – and I'm scared, for I'm nobody's child.

The bang of the door, the turn of the key
The mind doesn't function, this cannot be me.
Someone will come, it's a game, it's not real.
I'll try not to show the panic I feel
For I'm locked up in prison, hated, reviled,
I'm lonely, alone, and I'm nobody's child.

I'm beaten, exhausted, I feel sick with fear,
I'm cornered, confused, for there's nobody here
Who will hug me and hold me and give me some hope.
This place is hell, I don't think I can cope –
I feel filthy and tainted, disgusting, defiled,
No-one will love me; I'm nobody's child.

I'm finished with anger, aggression and strife
There's nothing to live for, I've hated my life
I've no more bravado, no tears left to cry.
I'm only sixteen and I now want to die.
They will close my case-history – all neatly filed
And no-one will mourn; for I'm nobody's child.

I have been concerned about children and young people in prison for over 30 years, ever since I saw a BBC Panorama programme about Feltham Young Offenders Institution in 1991. I was horrified by what I saw. The way these children, for that is what they are, were being treated was unbelievably brutal. Yes they were boys who had extremely problematic childhoods but the way they were being pushed and shoved and beaten and shouted at shocked me to the core. My own children were teenagers at the time and I kept thinking that there but for the grace of God and some frantic parenting could have gone either of them.

It was at that point that I became a member of The Howard League for Penal Reform.

So what exactly are Young Offender Institutions and what are they like?

There are many places where you will find answers to this question but I go to 'Politics Home' who give a very good over-all description.

They say that "Young Offender Institutions are prisons for 15-21 year olds and Feltham is one of the best known. They are run by the Prison Service as part of the prison estate as a whole. There are three forms of youth custody in the United Kingdom, Young Offender Institutions (which account for 73% of those in custody), Secure Training Centres (housing 17%) and Local Authority Secure Children's Homes (10%).

"Compared to other parts of the youth justice system, Young Offender Institutions have a lower staff to offender ratio, reflecting the focus of these institutions on incarceration as opposed to rehabilitation and care. They are also generally larger than other parts of the system. Critics of Young Offenders Institutions argue that imprisonment is totally inappropriate for young people."

'Politics Home' goes on to say that *"The majority of those within the institutions are said to have complex educational, social and often mental health needs, which critics say are often not addressed. Lack of resources and intimidating atmospheres are said to hamper rehabilitation work in Young Offenders Institutions. Indeed, some critics argue that the effect of incarceration has the opposite effect: with little to occupy them and in the company of other offenders, detainees may be put on the road to a life of crime."*

Then we have some statistics. *"The 2018/19 reoffending statistics showed that over two-thirds (69%) of children and young people released from custody reoffend within 12 months of release. They committed an average of 5 new offences per reoffender. This compares with a reoffending rate of 48% from adult prisons. A number of modern Young Offender Institutions have attracted particular criticism for their violence and disorder problems."*

They also strongly criticise the use of physical restraint and quote from a Joint Committee on Human Right's report which was published in **2019**. This Committee concluded that there was substantial medical evidence of the physical and psychological impacts of restraint particularly when used on children. They stated that *"restraint harms children, it harms staff, it undermines the objectives of detention, and contributes to a vicious circle of problems that can continue into the future. It found rates of restraint of children to be unacceptably high and said children's rights are being routinely breached."*

It really does make appalling reading, but then, two years later we hear from the former HM Chief Inspector of Prisons, Sir David Ramsbotham, who in **2021** condemned Feltham Young Offender Institution as *"one of the worst"* prisons in the system, with *"Dickensian conditions, racism and violence."*

As Frances Crook, former Chief Executive of the Howard League for Penal Reform, says: *"Various iterations of prisons for children as places of education and rehabilitation, have simply never worked."*

So those are some bare facts but the detail and the changes over the years are also important and I have been following them closely. I have signed up to receive the reports on YOIs by the prison inspectors from the Ministry of Justice and I have also written many letters to *The Times* newspaper as and when something particularly concerns me. There have been mountains of words written about this subject so I will need to be very circumspect with what I choose to highlight. But here we go.

I begin with my first letter about prisons which was published in *The Times* in July **1998**. Most YOIs are for boys only, so it appears difficult for the authorities to know what to do with girls.

Sir, It is very encouraging that the Home Office report 'Reducing Offending' *says that custody is no more successful in preventing criminal re-offending than are community penalties. At the moment there are about 80 girls between the ages of 15 and 17 in adult women's prisons. These already vulnerable and disadvantaged people are kept in conditions which are bound to have a harmful and corrupting influence.*

At a conference, held on July 21st in London by the Howard League for Penal Reform, Mr. Clive Fairweather, chief inspector for prisons in Scotland, said that the Scottish authorities were committed to having no girls of this age in their prisons by the millennium. When I asked Joyce Quin, Minister of State for Prisons and Probation, whether this was the aim of the Government in the rest of the UK, she said it was not.

These young girls, already victims themselves, would be better off in local authority secure units. Why is it not possible for this Government to be committed to removing them from such a damaging environment?

"Oh of course it is the fault of the parents" I hear people say when children get into trouble. And sometimes it most definitely is. Here is a letter from me which was published in *The Times* in January **2006.**

Sir The photograph of Chelsea O'Mahoney on the front page of The Times today (Jan 24th) is very disturbing. It is almost as though you are inviting us to look at her and hate her.

What she did (together with the others) was unbelievably appalling, ending with the death of an innocent man. However, unless we try to understand why more and more children (for that is what she was at the time of the attack) continue to behave in this way, these dreadful assaults will keep happening.

Chelsea, according to her defence lawyer, was virtually abandoned by her heroin addicted parents and left wandering the streets of London in the middle of the night at the age of 3. She was practically illiterate and, as the judge is reported as saying, her life 'lacks stability, consistency and effective boundaries and emotional care.'

What sort of society allows abandoned children to live like this? In some respects we have not progressed since the time of Dickens.

Well we really need to look at that last question and think about it carefully. Winston Churchill was fond of quoting the Russian writer and philosopher Dostoevsky who reportedly said that *"The degree of civilization in a society can be judged by entering its prisons."*

So come with me as we enter some prisons and test the veracity of that quotation.

We will continue with those prisons which hold young offenders.

What strikes me as so odd is that for years people have been saying that children who are locked up, for whatever reason, are children who need help and support, rather than severe and potentially damaging punishment.

The back stories of so many of these children are heartbreaking. We can go back to **1995** when the human rights lawyer, Helena Kennedy chaired an inquiry by the Howard League which investigated violence in young offenders' institutions. At that time she says that 40% of children in prison have been in local authority care. 90% have mental health or drug problems and many have suffered physical or sexual abuse. Too many also have severe literacy problems. As she says, *"Locking up children who have complex and multiple needs in worn down and neglectful institutions is not the answer."* It is so true also that if children were treated in such a way in any other environment it would trigger a child protection investigation.

This was all said in that inquiry in 1995. So how much have things improved?

Well here is the report from the Chief Inspector of Prisons which was presented to Parliament in **July 2023**.

HM Chief Inspector of Prisons for England and Wales Annual Report 2022–23

For the period 1 April 2022 to 31 March 2023

Presented to Parliament pursuant to Section 5A of the Prison Act 1952.

Ordered by the House of Commons to be printed on 5 July 2023

Young offender institutions (YOIs) are juvenile establishments that hold children under the age of 18. Other establishments hold young adults over the age of 18. Juvenile establishments are inspected annually.

"Outcome of previous recommendations in the YOIs reported on in 2022–23:

- *67% of our previous main/key concern recommendations in the area of safety had been achieved and 33% had not been achieved*
- *50% of our previous main/key concern recommendations in the area of care had been achieved and 50% had not been achieved*
- *60% of our previous main/key concern recommendations in the area of purposeful activity had been achieved and 40% had not been achieved*
- *57% of our previous main/key concern recommendations in the area of resettlement had been achieved and 43% had not been achieved."*

The report goes on to paint a picture where there had been a few improvements to life in these institutes but where there are still too many which fail abysmally in their treatment of vulnerable children.

The report then states:-

> **"Daily life is generally not child-friendly.**
>
> *Accommodation at many YOIs was not designed for children; in particular, the very large living units at Werrington and Wetherby were institutional and did not support effective relationships or behaviour management. The lack of private rooms at Cookham Wood and Feltham also hindered children's access to interventions and activities.*
>
> *Cleanliness had improved across most sites; most notably at Parc; communal areas had been kept clean, equipment was in good condition and well maintained, and staff encouraged and helped children to keep their cells clean. Parc seems to do quite well in most areas.*
>
> *But most children continued to eat all their meals alone in their cells. Again the exception was Parc where children enjoyed eating their meals together, and staff sat or ate with them at mealtimes. Feltham had also started doing this on a rota, although most meals continued to be eaten in cell.*
>
> *The introduction of laptops for every child was a very good initiative. YOIs had moved towards an electronic system for children to make applications for day-to-day services, and the laptops were set up to provide helpful information, make applications or raise complaints, and enable children to check their prison shop spending themselves without relying on staff to do it."*

There were reports on health and on diversity in various places but the most worrying issue is that too much time is still spent locked up in their cells.

"Purposeful activity.

The report says that *"After five Independent Reviews of Progress (IRPs) during the year, we found that reasonable progress had been made against only one of five recommendations about the time children spent out of their cells. No YOI met our expectation that children should be unlocked for 10 hours a day. Parc came the closest with between eight and 11 hours on weekdays. Regimes were more limited at the other four YOIs, offering up to 6.5 hours unlocked on weekdays at Feltham, six hours at Cookham Wood and Wetherby, and 5.5 hours at Werrington. Weekends were worse at all five sites with an average of between three and six hours out of cell on Saturdays and Sundays.*

However, delivery of these regimes was inconsistent and some children experienced very little time out of cell. Staff difficulties at all sites, except Parc, resulted in regime curtailments that restricted children's time unlocked. This often affected the evening and weekend activities that supported relationship-building with staff and peers, and children's well-being. Conflicts between children could further limit time out of cell."

So Parc appears to be offering the best regime albeit from a very low bar but we need to look further at Cookham Wood, Feltham and Wetherby.

COOKHAM WOOD

On 27th April **2023** the Chief Inspector of Prisons issued an Urgent Notification to the Secretary of State for Justice demanding immediate action to improve the conditions at the YOI Cookham Wood in Kent. This means that he has to reply within 28 days. Cookham Wood had been placed in emergency measures in April.

Apparently children felt unsafe here and were resorting to carrying weapons. Many had been made by the boys who had scavenged metal from kettles and the like. The prison was dirty and uncared for and the staff were exhausted and felt unsupported by senior managers.

Charlie Taylor, the Chief Inspector of Prisons said: *"Many of these children have committed serious crimes and have rightly been detained. Nevertheless, they are still children, many of whom have come from difficult backgrounds. They ought to be receiving education and support to make better choices in the future, supporting their rehabilitation and growth into adulthood so they leave custody in a better position than they entered it. We spoke to boys who'd had almost no human contact at all in days, and who had resorted to trying to stick up photos of home with toothpaste on the walls of the tiny cells that became their whole world. Such treatment of children is appalling. This is a scandal and it cannot be allowed to continue."*

In May the government approved a series of urgent measures in a crackdown on weapons at Cookham Wood. The then Prisons Minister Damian Hinds said: *"Cookham Wood is home to some of society's most troubled children, many with violent convictions, but the situation there is completely unacceptable as it is preventing us from helping these young offenders turn their backs on crime. That is why we have already appointed a new governor to provide stronger leadership and started a review into how children were being separated to prevent violence but it is clear further action is needed. Last month's inspection found unacceptable failings at HMYOI Cookham Wood, and today I am setting out how we will put this right without delay.*

Children should feel safe in custody and leave in a better state than when they entered it. These measures to tackle gang violence and improve education will make sure we can rehabilitate these children and reduce their risk of reoffending."

But then in **July 2023** Mr. Taylor's team found the conditions at Cookham Wood had deteriorated and were now of *"considerable concern"*.

Members of the 360-strong team of staff were described as *"demoralised"* and *"frightened"*, with some seeming to have *"given up"* and no longer even wearing the correct uniform to work.

Some of the 24 senior bosses *"stayed out of sight in their offices,"* according to the watchdog.

As he called for *"urgent, concerted and long-term commitment"* from prison leaders to improve standards, Mr. Taylor said: *"These findings would be deeply troubling in any prison, but given that Cookham Wood holds children, they were completely unacceptable.*

"As a result, I had no choice but to write to the secretary of state immediately after the inspection and invoke the urgent notification process."

The Prison Reform Trust described the report as *"shocking"* and said it revealed a *"failure of leadership at the highest levels of the youth justice system"*.

Then on the **6th October 2023** Staff working at Cookham Wood, called on the government to allow them to use PAVA spray to better protect themselves from these violent children.

I really cannot believe they would use this incapacitating spray on young people in prison.

PAVA spray is far more toxic than CS gas and is primarily aimed at the eyes causing severe pain, a burning sensation on the skin and uncontrollable coughing.

The Howard League states that they have a principled objection to any approach that inflicts pain on someone deliberately, and this includes the use of PAVA spray. An instructor on a training video likens it to *"wet fire."*

Apparently in 2018 the government announced that PAVA spray would be rolled out to all male category A to D prisons but a decision on its further use was still being considered. Judith Feline, a former governor at Maidstone prison and ex-prison officer at Cookham Wood, was undecided on whether PAVA spray was the solution to cutting violence.

She told BBC South East: *"I don't know whether PAVA is the solution. I have seen it used in the adult estate and it has a pretty nasty effect on you, because your eyes run and it's very sore, but it stops you doing whatever you are doing.*

"There are all sorts of issues using that on children. They might be violent young men but they are kids, it's a very difficult decision to make," she added.

The Howard League goes on to say that *"it reflects a profound failure on the part of those responsible for children in custody that they would consider introducing weapons in the name of safety and it only underlines the fact that prison is no place for a child."*

So no Ms. Feline, I don't think it is a difficult decision. If we want prisons to be safe and positive places for already disadvantaged children then we need properly trained staff to take care of them.

And then we see this:

21st March 2024. *"Young offenders from HMYOI Cookham Wood will be transferred and the site repurposed as an adult prison under plans announced by the Ministry of Justice today (21 March 2024). In a bid to boost prison capacity the establishment will operate as an adult male prison as early as the summer, while options are being reviewed for its longer-term use. Young offenders currently housed at Cookham Wood will be moved to other sites across the secure youth estate to provide the continued support needed for them to turn their backs on crime for good.*

They will be moved on a case-by-case basis, taking into account their specific needs, views from other professionals and the need to maintain family ties. These transfers will be done in a supervised manner, in consultation with families and youth offending teams."

Well having read all the above I wish I could believe that. So that's the end of one Young Offenders' Institute.

But now we need to go back to **Feltham.**

And before we go any further we just need to remind ourselves of a *"shocking catalogue of failure"* when in the year **2000** there was a racist murder of an Asian teenager called Zahid Mubarek.

Zahid Mubarek was 19 years old and had been convicted of shoplifting £6 worth of goods from a supermarket. He was sentenced to serve ninety days at Feltham Young Offender Institution. He had had no previous convictions and his family had had no previous confrontations or records with the police either before Zahid's case. His grandfather had served in the Pakistan Army Corps of Engineers and in 1960, migrated with his family to East London. His father worked as a manager in a factory for 28 years in Manchester. They were a Muslim family. I absolutely do not understand this custodial sentence, of 90 days, for a first offence of stealing £6 worth of razor blades and interfering with a car.

But what is absolutely impossible to understand is why he was forced to share his cell with a known racist and career criminal. Apparently it was the last available bed but with the track record of Robert Stewart they should have been able to move others around. Stewart had 17 convictions for 80 offences and other prisons had reported that he had clear mental health issues and had been diagnosed as a psychopath in November 1999. But more than that, he was obsessed with the symbolism of fascism and had a deep-seated hatred of black and Asian people.

Reportedly the guard responsible for placing him with Mubarek had no idea who Stewart was or that he was a known racist, having not been given access to his security files. Actually Stewart had a cross and the letters 'RIP' tattooed on his forehead, which I would have thought would have been a slight clue.

Having been together for about a month Mubarek was trying to get some sleep before being released the following morning when at 3.35am on the 21st March 2000 Stewart took a table leg that he had already broken off the table two weeks earlier and battered his sleeping cellmate between seven and eleven times over the head. He then calmly pressed the alarm bell, said there had been an accident and when moved to another cell washed all blood and other evidence from his hands and clothes. However the give-away signs were the fact that the prison officers did see him standing over Mubarek covered in blood and holding a large table leg and he had also written a message on the wall of the cell he was moved to reading "*Just killed me padmate*", signed off with a swastika. Yes those are pretty big clues I would say. Mubarek died in hospital later that day.

This particular murder caused the most voluble outrage from everyone concerned with the conditions of our prisons. And I can't understand that either. There have been many deaths and murders in our prisons and they should all be causing outrage and shock.

In the murder trial it was stated that Zahid Mubarek died because of a combination of his cellmate's racism and failures of the Prison Service. So institutional murder I would think in a place where his parents thought he would be safe and maybe get some help with his burgeoning drug habit.

So I now go back a few years to check on general progress.

In 2015 a report about Feltham stated that 'Prison inspectors have highlighted "*serious concerns*" at one of London's young offenders' institutions, describing "*unpredictable and reckless*" violence.'

Staff at Feltham in west London were constantly trying to keep apart boys from more than 40 gangs. Inspectors found too many inmates were locked in cells for up to 23 hours a day, amounting to *"solitary confinement"*.

One member of staff told the BBC *"I was regularly seeing inmates attacked with weapons - pool balls, pool sticks, anything they could get their hands on. It was not uncommon to see someone on the floor getting their head stamped on by a large group."*

In 2017 The HM Inspectorate of Prisons (HMIP) gave YOI Feltham in west London its lowest judgement for safety after finding levels of *"very serious"* violence had risen.

IN 2019 safety levels at Feltham had dropped to an *"appalling"* level over the first half of the year, inspectors said. Inspectors had visited part of the prison known as Feltham A in July following an unannounced check in January.

Peter Clarke was the Chief inspector of prisons at this time and he highlighted his concerns to the justice secretary who was Robert Buckland. *"Fundamental change"* was required, he said as in six months, there had been a 45% rise in violence incidents, while levels of self-harm had tripled and the number of assaults against staff surged by about 150%.

Some 74% of children said they had been physically restrained there, while 40% claimed they had felt unsafe at some point during their stay.

So in August 2019, Justice Secretary Robert Buckland announced a series of pledges to improve standards at the prison.

Let's see how that has gone.

Here is some of the inspection report for **2023.**

Well, well here we go again.

"*After many years as a young offender institution (YOI) for 18–21-year olds, over the last year Feltham B has been re-rolled to become a category C training prison holding prisoners up to the age of 30, as well as continuing to hold sentenced young offenders aged 18–21 in response to national population pressure.*

"*This change increased their population by around 40%. The lack of planning meant there was not nearly enough work or education for the prison to deliver its function as a category C training prison. While a well-led offender management unit had worked hard to reduce large backlogs of work, their efforts were undermined by shortfalls in London probation and the increasing number of high risk men into the prison. The use of segregation was high and the unit was in poor condition, with a leaking roof, algae growth in the showers and filthy toilets.*

"*A lack of activity spaces, staff shortages and safety concerns among prisoners meant attendance at work was woeful, and just one in five prisoners was employed in activity off the wing. The prison's poor and unpredictable daily routine was often the cause of violence against staff.*"

So yet another YOI being compromised due to lack of adult prison spaces. This time no mention of moving young offenders. They will just have to mix with adult men some of whom are "*high risk.*"

So how is that all going?

The report finds that levels of violence were "*too high and prisoners had poor perceptions of their safety*".

"*Leaders, staff and prisoners were over-reliant on keeping prisoners apart rather than addressing underlying causes of violence. Investigations into incidents were often delayed and sometimes of poor quality,*" it said.

To sum it up: "*Despite the change in purpose, at the time of this visit Feltham B was not operating as a category C training prison where we would expect the whole population to be fully occupied. Instead, we found just one in five prisoners was gainfully employed in activity off the wing. Local leaders will be unable to make significant progress without substantial support from HMPPS leaders. This will need to focus on increasing the amount of work at the site, changing the culture and addressing the shortfalls in the probation service in London."* Charlie Taylor, HM Chief Inspector of Prisons, January 2024

So absolutely nothing has improved after a murder in 2000. It has got steadily more dangerous because no-one bothered to read those reports, or even worse, they were read but people chose not to do anything and instead, it has been given a change of category which will be detrimental and dangerous to the young people there and very likely continue on its downward spiral.

So now we go to Wetherby in West Yorkshire. I warn you that what we find here is absolutely appalling as well. This site holds around 240 *"extremely challenging young people"* aged between 15 and 18.

In a **2018/19** report the Independent Monitoring Board states that **'Urgent action is needed to tackle the causes of violent behaviour with** *"more and more"* **people going to young offender institutions.'**

So inspectors visited this YOI in **November and December 2023**. They said *"We wanted to find out if things were better, the same or worse for young people since we last visited in 2021."*

And I really welcome the list of things that they say they would like to happen.

- "We want girls to live somewhere that meets their needs.
- We want young people to be separated from others for less time.
- We want young people who are separated to get more time out of their cells
- We want staff to restrain young people only when they need to, and to do it safely.

- We want young people to have better support plans
- We want buildings to be repaired and broken things to be fixed.
- We want the heating to work properly.
- We want young people to have more time out of their cells, especially at weekends.
- We want English and maths teaching to be better.
- We want young people to get quicker replies if they complain about discrimination.
- We want waiting times for the dentist to be shorter."

Well these are lovely ambitions although they just re-emphasise the state of this prison. Mind you, regarding that last request, at the moment no-one can get an NHS dentist appointment inside or outside a prison.

They then say *"We will come back next year to check how well the YOI is doing. We will write a report to tell people what we find."*

Well that sounds very sensible.

So what did they find I wonder? Well it's not looking good.

A report dated the 7th March **2024** by the Children's Commissioner, Dame Rachel de Souza, comments on a report by the Chief Inspector of Prisons, Charlie Taylor, who discusses the treatment of a girl in Wetherby. At the time of this report there were 140 boys there aged between 15 and 18 and just **three girls**. I find this absolutely shocking even before I see what has happened to them.

Rachel de Souza is shocked and appalled by the fact that a girl had her clothes removed twice whilst under restraint by an all-male team of prison officers.

She writes that *"The same inspection report that failed Wetherby on the grounds of safety and failure to provide purposeful activity for the children in its care, also found instances of intrusive and traumatic strip-searching of girls, young people forced to live in freezing cold cells, and concerning use of 'pain-inducing techniques.'"*

She goes on to say that *"The failures documented in this report are quite clearly unacceptable and highlight two major issues: one about girls being kept in YOIs with inappropriate staffing and standards that do not meet their needs, and secondly the issue of YOIs more broadly not being fit for purpose.*

As Children's Commissioner, I have been sounding the alarm about the safety and conditions for children in custody, particularly those who are most vulnerable to risks like poor mental health or exploitation. I have deep concerns about these risks in YOIs – not only at Wetherby but at others around the country.

Simply put, this girl should not have been in a young offenders institute – she should have been in a secure setting that could support her needs effectively and safely."

In my book '**Our Lost Children**' I quote another report by Dame Rachel de Souza, which says that children as young as eight are being stopped and strip-searched by police. More than half of these took place without an appropriate adult present. A senior paediatrician has called for these kind of searches, those without an appropriate adult present, to be banned. Professor Andrew Bush writing in the 'Archives of Diseases in Childhood', which is the official journal of the Royal College of Paediatrics and Child Health, states that police should be subject to the same protocols as doctors. Unless they can justify their actions to an independent panel *"they should be dismissed and have to sign the sex-offender's register."*

He says that, *"As with an adult, removing someone's clothing without consent is sexual abuse".* This then, should also apply to prison officers.

And after all these years the Children's Commissioner says that *"I am really concerned about the lack of a national plan for the placement and care for these girls."*

She concludes her report by saying that *"Wetherby has the highest rates of self-harm incidents of any prison in the country, and the use of force against girls is very high. The report found that girls are frequently being strip searched, physically restrained, and having their clothing cut off and replaced with anti-ligature clothing. Earlier this week I wrote to the Justice Minister Alex Chalk to ask him how he is improving conditions since I last raised these concerns with him. My team and I will be visiting Wetherby as soon as possible to speak to the children there."*

She says *"We need more, smaller settings closer to where children live that can deliver education and therapeutic support safely. This needs to be done as a matter of urgency so more children aren't failed or put at risk."*

As Charlie Taylor said in this report *"care for vulnerable young people - especially girls - was "not good enough".*

He told the BBC that young offender institutions are too *"top heavy"*, with high numbers of middle-managers and *"frontline officers on the ground... leaving because of high levels of violence".*

He said *"there is no doubt these are difficult places to work"* and he called for *"real thinking"* on how to reduce violence in order to make youth justice more stable and sustainable.

The 'All Party Parliamentary Group on Women in the Penal System' has called on the government to rethink its policy and said: *"It has been known for many years that girls should not be in prison, so it is unacceptable that three have been placed in Wetherby because of failure at a national level to plan effectively."*

Indeed it has been known and said for years that girls should not be in prison at all. I refer you back to my letter to The *Times* at the beginning of this book which I wrote in **1998.**

But it was in 2021 that the girls in Wetherby were transferred there from the Rainsbrook Secure Training Centre in Warwickshire which after years of mis-management and severely critical reports was eventually 'mothballed' as they call it. I describe this centre in my previous books **'Beneath the Bluster'** and **'Behind the Headlines'** and finally after a complete meltdown the then Minister for Justice Robert Buckland obviously decided correctly that it was so dreadful and completely beyond help that it should be closed and the inmates sent elsewhere. So this is how a few girls ended up in Wetherby, a male prison for young offenders. It was once again due to the lack of care, lack of progress and lack of humanity at a YOI which had to be closed. So young people, once again, are just shunted around to the least worst option. But who on earth decided that a male prison was a good idea for three girls especially a prison with *"extremely challenging young people"*? There are other options available.

On the 21st March **2024**, John Drew of the Prison Reform Trust and former Chief Executive of the Youth Justice Board wrote a very interesting and informative blog. He explains that there are in fact very few girls in custody and he asks the same question. *'Why,'* he asks, *'are we placing a very small number of girls, acknowledged by the YCS as being "at very high risk of serious harm, in a boy's prison?"'*

He goes on to explain how girls in custody usually have very different needs to boys and they should be accommodated together in Secure Children's Homes.

He also states that on the night the girls were moved to Wetherby there were probably enough places in other Secure Children's Homes already paid for including Oakhill Secure Training Centre.

He concludes his blog by saying *"We need to say loud and clear, that girls should not be held in boy's prisons. To imprison them in this way shames us all."*

I really cannot understand how this needs saying. I do not have strong enough words to describe how I feel about this.

We are only a few days away from a general election and I think that Alex Chalk will not be giving too much time up at the moment to think about the state of our prisons. In fact I would be very surprised if he needs to think about them ever again.

But now I just need to check out **Oakhill Secure Training Centre** to where John Drew thinks girls could be sent.

This centre provides accommodation for up to 80 children, male and female, aged 12 to 19 years, who are serving a custodial sentence or who are remanded to custody by the courts. The most recent inspection was held on the 5th and 6th **March 2024**. Reading this report actually lifted my spirits.

There are recommendations for improvement but the very first sentence says, *"We did not identify any serious or widespread concerns in relation to the care or protection of children at this assurance inspection."*

Oh my word that sounds wonderful. To think there are 12 year olds here. My only concern was that at the time of this inspection, (ready for this?) out of 67 children there was only one girl. Unbelievable.

However I pick out just a few points from this report which give a flavour of the general environment here.

> *"Leaders remain passionate and committed to providing a safe and stable environment for children in Oakhill.*
>
> *The learning from the last inspection has been embraced and the centre is making solid and steady progress against most recommendations to improve children's experiences in Oakhill*
>
> *Children are able to form trusting relationships with the staff. Interactions are relaxed, with spontaneous expressions of fondness such as fist bumps and handshakes when meeting each other. Children reported that they have a number of staff to whom they can address any worries or concerns.*

Complaints are taken seriously. Investigations are resolved in a timely way and the reasons behind any findings clearly explained to children.

The Youth Custody Service (YCS) has consulted with children and, as a result, has provided funding leading to the purchase of new gym equipment. Children are using the new equipment, and the YCS plans to meet with the children in the near future to get their feedback

Children's health needs are well promoted

New staff are well supported through a structured training programme and the extension of senior leadership mentoring provides enhanced help and guidance."

So you see it **can** be done. But please place the girl in a different category secure unit as a matter of urgency.

But also in 2023 there was a report about children on remand. This was a joint thematic inspection led by HM Inspectorate of Probation and was published on **November 23rd 2023**

At any given time, there are around 200 to 250 children remanded in youth detention. But this report found that many of these children could have been safely managed in the community as many had no previous convictions. Some of the remands were for longer than a year which is hugely excessive.

They were also remanded in areas very far from their homes which makes it so much harder for visits from families and for them to keep in touch which is seen as vitally important for their general welfare.

So all this is **before** they have been tried in court or sentenced and in fact many of them will not go forward to receive a prison sentence at all. So they are experiencing prison in this way when it is completely unnecessary as was the boy in *'Nobody's Child'*.

So to return to Helena Kennedy, as she so rightly says in her book 'Just Law', *"the conditions experienced by thousands of children sent to prison each year should shame us all."*

But do they? Just to remind you she wrote this book in **2004** and from what we have read above, would indicate that there is still a long way to go.

Indeed there is, for I read today, (**16th June 2024**) in a small column in *The Times,* some remarks by Charlie Taylor Chief Inspector of prisons. We are back to Feltham, that young offender institution which caused me to become a member of the Howard League for Penal Reform over 30 years ago. The headline reads *"Child prison is most violent in Britain."*

The prison was inspected in March this year and he said he was *"very concerned"* at how much it had deteriorated in the past two years. Figures indicated that there was six times more violence in this prison than at one of the most violent adult jails in England and Wales. If you remember, there are children aged 15 in this prison.

On looking up this report I read more detail.

> *"Feltham A, in Greater London, manages children on remand and those who have been convicted by courts. The prison held 84 children at the time of inspection,"*

> *This means of course that some of these children are not guilty or will not receive a custodial sentence when their trial comes to court.*

> *"Incidents of disorder had tripled since the last inspection and the use of force, usually in response to violence, had risen by 68%. The situation was so volatile that some children said they did not want their families to visit in case violence broke out in front of them."*

Definitely not a safe environment in which to put any children.

"Inspectors found ongoing concerns about children's access to education, with the use of 266 keep-apart instructions. This meant that, rather than being placed in lessons with children who had similar abilities and interests, boys were allocated to classes based on whom they could mix without fighting."

Then *"Another major concern was the worryingly prolonged segregation of some children from their peers. Seven children had been separated for more than 50 days, two of them for more than 100."*

This sounds like some sort of torture chamber. I'm struggling for words to express my fury.

And then I read *"but it is to the credit of the governor and her leadership team that there were signs that they had managed to arrest this decline."*

I find it hard to correlate this remark with the findings of this report which show no improvement since the last report which was an unannounced inspection in January **2023.**

So it is absolutely clear that most YOIs have continued on a downward path since time began and Elizabeth Fry and John Howard would be appalled. There are many amazing charities working really hard on behalf of 'young offenders' but they are fighting against all odds.

The new prisons minister, James Timpson, is a small light in this darkness but there is a huge, almost overwhelming task ahead. So I say to the new Justice Secretary please look at the treatment of young people in the criminal justice system. If they were treated in this way anywhere else in our society the perpetrators would be arrested.

WOMEN IN PRISON

I return to the remarks by Cherie Blair with which I began this book. If you remember, she called for fewer women to be sent to prison. She also called for the end of pregnant women being sent to jail.

As I said we can go back to Elizabeth Fry in **1813** and ever since then prison reformers have been saying exactly the same as Cherie Blair who was speaking in **2024.**

Over and over again we hear it being said that many women should not be in prison at all. And I actually said it extremely clearly on the **14th January 1999** when my letter was published in the *Guardian*.

> *Sir. Even before Jack Straw's announcement of mandatory prison sentences for persistent burglars our prison population had been steadily rising. We are locking up more people than at any time since the beginning of the century and the female prison population is rising faster. More women than men are given custodial sentences for first offences.*
>
> *Most are for handling stolen property or for fine default, eg for not having a TV licence. They are certainly not a threat to the public. Many of these women are already vulnerable and victims of extreme poverty or physical abuse, and well over half of these women are mothers of young children and so they too are made to suffer. Two-thirds of all women on remand are eventually released into the community as innocent or given non-custodial sentences. It would be far more constructive (and*

cheaper) to deal with these women outside prison. Most of them need help rather than the bullying and drug-ridden regime of an adult prison.

And this is a letter of mine which was published in the year **2000** in *The Times.* This was written after a young woman had committed suicide whilst on remand.

Sir. The main way to stop the ever-increasing rate of prison suicides is to stop committing so many people to prison. Custodial sentencing should be kept as a last resort and given only to people who are a real threat to society.

Of the 91 people who took their own lives in prison last year nearly two–thirds were on remand. One was a young woman of 21 who was awaiting sentence after being convicted for driving without tax or insurance. She was in a single cell in Holloway and recovering from an addiction to hard drugs. Locking away a vulnerable young woman like this is medieval and barbaric.

This Government, however, is intent on building more and more prisons. It costs the taxpayer an enormous amount of money to keep people in prison and there will never be enough money to resource them properly. There are many alternative forms of sentencing. So long as courts continue to commit more and more people to prison the suicide rate will continue to rise.

Then another in **2001**

Sir. Your leading article today must have dismayed prison reformers. Prison may well incapacitate criminals by keeping them away from the public, but what happens when they are released? Most prisoners reoffend within months of being let out of prison. What exactly is the point of this? Prison is not a sensible option apart from the core of hardened and violent prisoners and it should be kept as a last resort, especially for women.

Imprison the woman and you punish her family. Most women in prison are mothers and by depriving them of their liberty you leave children uncared for. Most of these women are victims themselves—of neglect, of poverty, of abuse. A civilised society would give them help, not incarcerate them.

And one more in **2018**

Prison reformers have been campaigning for decades to try to keep most women offenders out of prison for all the reasons she mentions. And it is nonsense to say there isn't enough money for these residential centres and community services. Five new women's prisons have been scrapped and as it costs over £30,000 to keep one person in prison for one year it will be much cheaper to keep as many women as possible out of prison. And the report by the Chief Inspector of Prisons about drugs and violence being the norm in prisons today makes dreadful reading. Winston Churchill once said that you can judge a society by the state of its prisons. If that is so, then our society is not as civilised as we might like to think.

So obviously, as we will see, letters to the papers make not a scrap of difference. However, everyone involved in prison reform knows, by now, that most women in prison should quite simply not be there and that most of them are actually victims themselves. Helena Kennedy in her book "*Just Law*" written in **2004** states it really clearly.

She writes about the woman's prison, Holloway, in north London and says that "*the same issues arise repeatedly: appalling family circumstances, histories of neglect, abuse and sexual exploitation, poor health, mental disorders, lack of support, inadequate housing or homelessness, poverty and debt and little expectation of change. Many women have themselves been victims of crime, usually violence within the home or sexual violence when they were children. Poor, battered and abused, they find themselves continually punished.*"

But of course you hear the popular press shouting from the roof-tops that we, the law-abiding innocent public, need to be protected from these criminals so they should be locked up. So let us look at some facts.

Most women entering prison are there for non-violent offences. Their crimes are mainly theft, handling stolen goods, supporting some-ones else's drug use or for non-payment of council tax or television licence. In her book "*Invisible Women*" Angela Devlin writes that a senior Holloway governor told her: "*I could release nearly all of the 500 women in the prison tomorrow, and there would not be a crime wave in London. But the problem is convincing politicians, the public and the media of that.*"

Oh my goodness what a truism is that. She wrote her book in **2004** and we are still writing about it all today in **2024.**

Then there is no rehabilitation going on in our prisons and again this applies particularly to women because they generally get short sentences which leaves no time for education or therapy of any kind. To quote the Prison Reform Trust: "*Over half (58%) of prison sentences given to women in 2022 were for less than six months, despite a widespread recognition that short prison sentences are harmful and ineffective.*"

As we know, even a few weeks in custody can be enough to cause a woman to lose her job, her home and her children.

There have been reports, after reports, after reports, debates, articles, and discussions year, after year, after year, about what should be done with our prison system, and in particular with women in prison, that by now our prisons should be models of excellence.

So let's have a look at some of these reports.

In **2007 The Corston Report** was published and talked so much sense that we all thought a change was imminent.

Baroness Corston describes how her interest in women in the criminal justice system goes back many years. She said *"the first time I visited Holloway prison I was shocked at the reality of prison life, at the life stories of some of the women in prison and, above all, will never forget my first sight of a baby in prison."*

She states the problems clearly and I quote a few of her words in her introduction.

> *"I do not believe, like some campaigners, that no women should be held in custody. There are some crimes for which custody is the only resort in the interests of justice and public protection, but I was dismayed to see so many women frequently sentenced for short periods of time for very minor offences, causing chaos and disruption to their lives and families, without any realistic chance of addressing the causes of their criminality."*

> *"The effects on the 18,000 children every year whose mothers are sent to prison are so often nothing short of catastrophic. I have concluded that the nature of women's custody in many of our prisons needs to be radically rethought."*

> *"There are many women in prison, either on remand or serving sentences for minor, non-violent offences, for whom prison is both disproportionate and inappropriate. Many of them suffer poor physical and mental health or substance abuse, or both. Large numbers have endured violent or sexual abuse or had chaotic childhoods. Many have been in care. I have concluded that we are rightly exercised about paedophiles, but seem to have little sympathy, understanding or interest in those who have been their victims, many of whom end up in prison. The tragic series of murders in Suffolk during December 2006 rightly focused public attention on these women as women first and foremost - someone's daughter, mother, girlfriend, then as victims – exploited by men, damaged by abuse and drug addiction. These are among the women whom society must support and help to establish themselves in the community."*

So of course she fully understands the problems and she makes many recommendations. But one of the most important was the need to build small units around the country in order to detain the small number of women that should have custodial sentences. That would result in women being nearer their families and so maintaining contact with them. It would mean that individual programmes would be easier to instigate and the different requirements that women need to men could be implemented.

She talks about the public perception of prisoners.

> *"There is some research evidence that suggests that, while the public are critical of sentencers that they see as being too lenient, there is also support for treating rather than punishing underlying problems. A Mori poll conducted in 2003, for example, reported that over half the public surveyed thought that the best way of dealing with prison overcrowding was to build more residential centres so that drug addicted offenders could receive treatment. The same survey found that there was some evidence that the public's ambivalence towards non-custodial penalties related to a lack of knowledge about what they involve."*

There were already four pilot custodial centres which she welcomed.

> She said *"More funding must be made available immediately to extend the network of centres across the country. I appreciate that this cannot happen overnight and a programme needs to be drawn up by the new Commissioner for Women who offend or are at risk of offending. As community centres for women are developed there will be scope to re-role the existing women's prisons for men, for whom generally they were originally built."*

We were all very buoyed up by this as there was a cross-party agreement to act on her recommendations.

Altogether there were 43 recommendations in a long and very detailed review.

But then we hear that two of the recommendations were not accepted by the government one of which was, *"The government should announce within six months a clear strategy to replace existing women's prisons with suitable, geographically dispersed, small, multi-functional, custodial centres within 10 years"* This was a huge disappointment and as a result, no government strategy was announced within the six months following the publication of the report. Instead the government announced that it was building new and large community prisons. So this brilliant idea by the Corston report was ignored to the detriment of women everywhere.

Then I read in Hansard a debate in the House of Lords entitled **'Women: Custodial Sentencing.'** This was held on the 26th June **2014** and was called 'question for a short debate'.

Indeed it lasted just one hour.

Baroness Healey of Primrose Hill had called for this debate and said she was quoting the Prison Reform Trust. It was an important debate and I pick out the most relevant comments.

She began by saying that: " *Women in prison are 10 times more likely than men to harm themselves, most women are in prison for short periods and they have very high reconviction rates, which demonstrate that for many women prison is neither rehabilitative nor a deterrent."*

She went on to say that: *"There is a growing consensus that most of the solutions to women's offending lie outside prison walls in treatment for addictions and mental health problems, protection from domestic violence and coercive relationships, secure housing, debt management, education, skills development and employment. Community services enable women to take control of their lives, care for their children and address the causes of their offending."*

She identifies a report from Barnardo's called, '**On the Outside: Identifying and Supporting Children with a Parent in Prison,**' which estimates that 200,000 children are affected by the imprisonment of a parent, with an increased likelihood of facing family breakdown, poverty and isolation.

It just seems to me to be a no-brainer. Prisons were built for men and whilst there are also many men who should not be there, so far as women are concerned prisons are completely unsuitable for most women.

In fact Lord Ramsbotham speaks in this debate and I am shocked by what he had to say about the different approach to men.

"One thing that I shall never forget" he says *"is finding on my initial inspection of Holloway that women's injuries were recorded on a diagram of a man's body, as there were no diagrams of female bodies available in the Prison Service. After I had walked out of Holloway, the Government produced an action plan for that prison, which I supervised by annual inspections, to see how it was being maintained. That was fine while the action plan lasted but, after it had finished, there was nothing. So Holloway has zigzagged up and down, as have all other women's prisons ever since."*

Much earlier in his book *'Prisongate'* written in **2003** we hear of women telling him how they were put in chains whilst in labour. He could not believe what he heard and saw when inspecting Holloway women's prison in December **1995**. Many of the women were in their cells all day, and all he could hear as he walked through the corridors were shouts, sobs, people kicking doors and the banging of someone's head against a wall.

He was disgusted by it and said that *"by any normal standards of responsibility and accountability I believe the governor and the senior medical officer should be sacked. But in fairness so should those in Prison Service Headquarters who not only allowed what I had seen to take place but also to continue unchecked."* He wrote *"What I had seen in Holloway was an affront to human decency that was wholly unworthy of a civilised society."*

Michael Howard was the Home Secretary and Ramsbotham was shocked that he had appeared to have done nothing about any of this. I'm not though. I met Michael Howard one day in the 1990s when I was walking through the shopping mall in Watford. There was a lot about women in prison in the media at the time. There he was with his entourage also walking through the mall and so I thought here is my chance. I went up to him and said *"Hello Mr. Howard."* He turned and smiled at me and asked me how I was. I think he thought that I looked like a pleasant middle-aged, middle-class woman and probably a Conservative voter. So I said to him *"Mr. Howard what are you going to do about the women in prison who really should not be there?"*

My word his demeanor changed rapidly. He glowered at me and said *"if they've done something wrong they should be in prison."* I tried to reason with him but he just kept repeating this mantra, *"If they've done something wrong they should be in prison."* We were walking really quickly by this point and I was having to keep up with him. Looking back it was quite funny but at the time I thought he was extremely rude. As I drew back a member of his team turned to me rather embarrassed, gave me his card and said *"do feel free to get in touch with me if you would like to discuss this further."*

So David Ramsbotham was also fed up with him and ends his chapter on Holloway saying that *"The memory of those days will be with me forever. More immediately they set my agenda for the next five years."*

So we go on to the **"Ministry of Justice Strategic Objectives for Female Offender –GOV. UK March 2013"**

Helen Grant MP heads a new ministerial team within the Ministry of Justice and she says that *"we have already started work on reforming the rehabilitation of offenders and addressing the failings in our youth custodial estate to break the depressing cycle of reoffending. We must now look more carefully at how we deal with female offenders. Many female offenders have a background of abuse, and first-hand experience of the care system."* She goes on to mention the many problems women have which we are all too familiar with and ends by saying:-

"I am absolutely committed to driving this forward across Government, and today have set out our strategic priorities. Together with the new expert Advisory Board I will convene, I want to develop policies to tackle female re-offending, to help women into gainful employment and safe environments, and off the 'conveyor belt to crime'. This can only be the right thing to do for women in the criminal justice system – and the right thing for their children, for their families and for society."

Wonderful words indeed.

Then: **"Government response to the Justice Committee's Second Report of Session 2013-14: Female Offender"**

"We welcome the 'Justice Select Committee's Report, Women Offenders: After the Corston Report'. Today we are setting out our new approach to managing female offenders. We are developing the custodial estate so that women can stay closer to home and maintain links with their families. We are establishing community employment regimes across the prison estate. These will enable women at the appropriate low-risk level to work out in the community so that they can build employment experience that they can continue on release."

They go on to say that:

*"We are setting up an open unit at **HMP Styal** which will accommodate 25 women who are assessed as being at the appropriate low-risk level. These women will be supported to work outside of the prison with access to the rehabilitative*

intervention programmes and health treatment available at the prison. We will test this approach. We will also explore the creation of further commercial employment opportunities in and around HMP Styal.

With these changes to the estate we are confident that the need for the two women's open prisons, in Yorkshire and Kent, will decline."

And also *"Simultaneously we will make each and every custodial establishment in the women's prison estate a resettlement prison and will support all women through-the-gate on release."*

Yet more fine words but we need to look at HMP Styal now in 2024 to see how successful it has been since it opened this special unit in 2015.

HMP Styal is the first prison to launch its open accommodation, with a house just outside the prison gates which will house up to 25 offenders. This is supposed to act as a stepping stone back into the community for female offenders.

Minister Simon Hughes said on the 29th January **2015**: *"The launch of the open accommodation at Styal is the first step of a vital reform we are making to the women's prison estate – helping female offenders prepare for their release by testing them in open conditions, and at the same time keeping them as close to home as possible. This will mean that before leaving custody, they can already start to make the local links they need on their release – such as finding job opportunities, housing, or other local services. These are essential factors to helping offenders turn away from crime and change their lives for good. All offenders being located in open conditions have been risk assessed and categorised as being of low risk to the public and a low risk of reoffending."*

My word. If the correct words improved prisons we would have the best and most effective prison system in the world.

Because I then see a report by BBC North West on HMP Styal open prison written by Scott Hesketh and Daniel O'Donoghue on the **21st March 2024**. It makes shocking reading and I quote some individual stories because I believe their voices should be heard.

We will go back to well before these new initiatives were introduced.

One young woman describes it as being *"hell on earth"*

There have been at least 11 suicides at HMP Styal in Cheshire since 2007 - more than any other women's jail in England. The youngest, Annelise Sanderson, was 18 when she was found dead in her cell in December 2020. She had been arrested in the summer of 2020 for stealing a pair of trainers and assaulting emergency workers who had intervened. On the day of her arrest, she poured petrol on herself and tried to drink it. Instead of being offered psychiatric treatment, she was subsequently sentenced to 12 months at Styal open prison.

Another inmate Francesca Barker-Mills was detained at HMP Styal for two months after being convicted of fraud in December 2020. *"The first thing that resonates with me was the screaming"* she said. *"There was blood spatter on the walls. It was horrible."* She describes the complete lack of help or support and says she had plenty of opportunities to kill herself.

Valerie Hayes was found hanged in her cell just 40 days into a second stretch at the prison in **May 2006**

In **2012** inspectors said conditions at Styal's mental health unit were *"more shocking and distressing than anything I have yet seen."*

But on it goes because an investigation is under way into the deaths of two more Styal prisoners just before Christmas in **2023** when Laura Parry, 59, and Sarah Jackson, 46, died within a week of each other.

I find it unbelievable that we allow this to happen in our prisons.

And the two open prisons in Yorkshire and Kent have not been closed. So the 2013/14 report has failed to deliver.

So what is the response from the government to this?

The government has said that following Annelise's death in 2020, they have tripled Styal's mental health budget to £1.5m. A Ministry of Justice spokesperson said: *"The number of women in prison has fallen considerably since 2010 and we are continuing to invest millions into community services to steer female offenders away from jail and help get their lives back on track. "However, for those women who judges decide must serve a prison sentence we are transforming the mental health support on offer in our jails, including tailored, round-the-clock care, extra face-to-face time with specialist staff and improved self-harm training for all frontline officers."*

But we see no evidence whatsoever in our prisons today. It is all just words. And as I say, some very fine words too. I even find some from Liz Truss.

These are in the **November 2016 Prison Safety and Reform White paper.**

She states that: *"Few of us see what goes on behind the high walls of our prisons. Though we don't know whether the offenders within are simply marking time or working hard to turn their lives around, we should all care. With a few exceptions, everyone who spends time in one of Her Majesty's prisons will one day be back in our community. However currently nearly half of all prisoners go on to re-offend within a year. This revolving door of crime and prison costs society £15bn a year. Prisons are not working. We will never be able to address the issue of re-offending if we do not address the current level of violence and safety issues in our prisons. That is why I am determined to make prisons work. This requires a huge cultural and structural change within our prisons – a transformation away from offender warehouses to disciplined and purposeful centres of reform where all prisoners get a second chance at leading a good life."*

Wow fine words indeed. Her own words? Not absolutely convinced about that.

You might remember that Truss was Secretary of State for Justice and Lord Chancellor at this time.

She concludes after 61 pages with: *"We will publish a strategy setting out how we will improve the safety and reform of female offenders in custody and in the community in early 2017."* Aha, so how did that go?

Well she only lasted in that post another six months so as I didn't hear any more I wrote to the Ministry of Justice in **December 2017** stating some of my concerns about the prison system. I had a reply in **January 2018**. It was a long and detailed reply and I quote just part of it.

They write: *"We have made substantial progress against the commitments outlined in the November 2016 Prison Safety and Reform White Paper. We will always have enough prison capacity for those committed by the courts and will aim to manage the prison population in a way that gives tax payers the best possible value for money. Our prison estate reforms will benefit prisoners with mental health concerns through replacing up to 10,000 old and unsuitable places with modern and fit for purpose ones and through reconfiguration."*

Well I just pause here to challenge them on this. It is **2024** and our prisons are actually so full that they are close to breaking point. The total population stands at 87,453 with a *"usable operational capacity"* of 88,864 and the newly elected Prime Minister highlighted overpopulation in prisons as one of his government's key issues to tackle. He actually said that the situation was far worse than he had been led to believe and the only option they have is to release prisoners early to free up accommodation. The government projects that the prison population will rise by a further 7,400 people to reach 93,200 by 2024—placing further pressure on places.

So these new prison places? Where are they? Well the Prison Reform Trust states that:-

> *"The government has committed to building 20,000 new prison places by the mid-2020s to meet rising demand. But just 5,202 places had been built by 5 June 2023. Even if all of the government's planned capacity projects are delivered on time there will still be a short fall of 2,300 prison places by March 2025. Nearly 10,700 prison places have been closed since 2010—many of them old and/or dilapidated. At the same time, nearly 11,000 places have been created, a net increase of just 300 prison places."*

They sound to me a bit like Boris's 40 new hospitals.

The email to me goes on to describe the new prison places saying they will be less noisy and have plenty of natural light and *"our reforms will intend to reduce crowding by around 20% and create the physical conditions for Governors to have better educational training and rehabilitation outcomes."*

They then address my concerns about the length of time prisoners stay in their cells. They say it can vary according to the level of staff etc. but *"All prisons are required to have systems in place to monitor regimes and ensure that they are safe, decent, secure and sustainable."*

Then we get to the females. *"We are developing a Female Offender Strategy as announced in the White Paper to improve outcomes for women in the community and in custody."*

Wait a minute. How will that differ from the Justice Committee's Second Report of Session **2013-14**: Female Offender?

"However," they say, *"considering how we can best address the needs of female offenders to improve outcomes for them, their families and their communities is a complex issue that we want to get right. So we are working hard to develop the strategy and we will publish it in due course."*

Well, well we get to see this Female Offender Strategy just 6 months later in June **2018.** It repeats everything that we all know already. It says that *"custody should be a last resort, reserved for the most serious offences."* It makes clear that, *"where appropriate, women should be given the support they need to address their offending behaviour in community settings, and that early intervention is essential to reduce the number of women entering the justice system. By taking a gender-informed approach, we want to improve the outcomes for female offenders at all points of the system."*

The strategy highlighted that many of these women are victims, as well as perpetrators of crime. And they set out specific and measurable commitments for **2022 to 2025,** with a focus on 4 aims:

1. Fewer women entering the criminal justice system and reoffending.
2. Fewer women serving short custodial sentences with a greater proportion managed successfully in the community.
3. Better outcomes for women in custody.
4. Protecting the public through better outcomes for women on release."

Oh goodness they could have got all of this from Elizabeth Fry.

So how is this working out? Well in the **January 2023 Female Offender Strategy Delivery Plan 2022–2025** they have exactly the same 4 commitments as we see above. This would imply that nothing has moved forward in the last six years. They have 35 pages saying what they have done and are doing but we see the words *"developing"*, and *"publishing"* and *"reviewing"* and from what I see I am afraid it is not enough. There has been no development, no publishing and no reviewing that I can see.

Indeed a report from the Ministry of Justice says that the women's prison population on 6th October 2023 was 3,604- a rise of 15% since January- that is almost 500 women. They are predicting a rise to 3.800 by November 2024.

And according to the Prison Reform Trust only half of women left prison with settled accommodation in the year to March 2023. There is at the moment no reduction in short sentences for women although this issue is addressed in a sentencing bill that was put before parliament just before parliament went into recess before the general election.

So many words, so many recommendations, so much anger and distress, yet the anguish and inhumanity go on.

And it is impossible to talk about women in prison without realising that many, if not most, are mothers. Some will have left their children at home, some will have their babies with them, and some, to our everlasting shame, will have babies born to them whilst in a prison cell.

There are many countries which prohibit the sending of pregnant women and mothers of infants to prison. They include, Italy, Portugal, the Russian Federation, Ukraine, Georgia, Brazil, Mexico and Colombia. But the UK is not one of them.

Everyone concerned about pregnant women in prison will remember the appalling situation which I describe at the beginning of my book '**Behind the Headlines**'. A young woman, who was 18 years old, was in a prison cell, when she goes into labour and calls for help, but none is forthcoming. She calls again and again but eventually gives birth on her own without any medical assistance whatsoever. Her baby is purple and not breathing and she has to bite through the umbilical cord and then wraps the baby in a towel. 12 hours later, after two prisoners called for help, prison staff entered her cell to find the place covered in blood and her under the duvet with her dead baby.

Another mother told her story about being taken belatedly to hospital in handcuffs for the birth of her baby having had no help, support or kindness from any of the staff throughout the 3 last months of her pregnancy, only from the other female prisoners.

This was in **Bronzefield** prison near Ashford in Surrey. It is the only purpose-built private prison solely for women in the UK, and is the largest female prison in Europe. The prison is operated by Sodexo Justice Services. Its annual report and accounts for **2017/18** show the cost per prisoner at Bronzefield is £66,294, at least £10,000 higher than any other women's prison.

The Prisons and Probation Ombudsman reported many failings in the way the 18 year old was treated. Nobody came though the prisoner pressed her bell twice and asked for a nurse. The Ombudsman, Sue McAllister said: '*Ms. A gave birth alone in her cell overnight without medical assistance. Overall the healthcare offered to her was not equivalent to that she could have expected in the community. Prison staff on the mother's block did not know that the birth was imminent and health agencies did not share information adequately with the prison. The mother was vulnerable, it was her first time in prison, and she was on remand facing a robbery charge. It was alleged she had "a troubled and traumatic childhood" and was "sad, angry and scared" after she was told the baby would be taken away at birth.*'

I need to remind you that we are talking about the UK in the 21st century.

The Howard League has repeatedly called for pregnant women and mothers with small children to be given non-custodial sentences. When Francis Crook was their Director she was saying back in the **1990s** that "*We should be petitioning judges not to send women with children to prison at all. I would prefer all prisons to refuse to take in babies under the Children Act. Then something would have to be done. There needs to be a stand on principle.*"

In **1998** the Prison Reform Trust announced that they had launched a major inquiry into women's imprisonment. One of the initiatives to be studied was "*integrating health services into a 'holistic service for women', to include a revision of the policy on pregnant women in prison and on prescribed medication levels.*"

Yet last year in **2023** over 25 years later, government figures showed that at least 194 women spent time in prison while pregnant, and 44 gave birth while being held in custody. They state *"We know that 40 women successfully applied to keep their baby in their care on a prison mother and baby unit but data on how many women are separated from babies because they're in custody are not available"*.

Not available? So they don't even know this dreadful statistic which means they certainly do not care.

I find it astonishing that pregnant women are still being sent to prison.

There are mother and baby units in some prisons but they are absolutely unacceptable. No child should be born in a prison cell and no mother should have to give birth whilst wearing handcuffs. I have already mentioned Sir David Ramsbotham's disgust when inspecting Holloway prison. He was in the mother and baby unit there when one woman asked *"Do you think it was right that I was in chains?"* Others repeated the question and he discovered they were all kept in chains during labour. When asking the governor why this was so she said it was a security requirement.

Any mothers reading this will be wondering at which point exactly during labour and the giving of birth would you be contemplating making a dash for it. As we see over and over again, prisons are designed by men for men with women tagged along as and when.

There are six prisons in England with mother and baby units and a mother can keep her baby with her for the first 18 months.

But of course if a woman is pregnant her health care in prison is severely compromised. A lack of appropriate maternity facilities and staffing puts women in prison at significant risk of pre-term labour, missed midwifery appointments, and without appropriate support for mothers and young children dealing with the severe impact of separation.

Labour continues to be an especially high risk point. Previous findings from the Nuffield Trust revealed in **2017/18**, show that just over 1 in 10 births by women in prison took place outside a hospital setting, meaning they gave birth either in a prison cell or on the way to the hospital.

I quote again from the Nuffield Trust just a few points from a report which they published in **2022**. It refers to the year **2019 -2020**. The author and Nuffield Trust Senior Research Fellow Dr. Miranda Davies said:

> *"Women in prison are almost twice as likely to go into preterm labour or delivery (11%) proportionately compared to the general population (6.5%).*
>
> *"Women in prison are almost twice as likely to miss obstetric appointments as the wider population, with 31.5% of appointments missed compared to 16.8% in the wider population.*
>
> *"Midwifery appointments were also missed by a slightly greater proportion of the prison population (21.5% compared to 16%).*
>
> *"Just under 45% of all outpatient appointments for women were missed in 2019/20. Missed appointments are a long-standing issue with access to health care services in prison and show little signs of improvement. Challenges remain likely to be a symptom of wider problems the prison estate faces, particularly staff availability."*

So, unsurprisingly, a pregnant woman in prison does not receive the same health care that she would elsewhere.

But then I read, from a few different sources, views which completely astound me.

Some are saying that a mother and baby unit in a prison can offer mothers an opportunity to bond with their baby in a more stable environment than usual. They say that the staff can provide a vital source of support for mothers, a secure base from which they can turn over a new leaf and begin a life away from crime. For some women they say this may be the first time they have experienced a nurturing attachment.

To which I say I do not believe that any mother would write this.

This is a PRISON which we are talking about here.

Do we really mean that in England in **2024** we think a woman will get better treatment for her and her new born baby in a prison? Do we really think that the staff ratio is sufficient to provide constant support and care? Do we really think that the prison environment is more suitable for a baby and then a toddler? Do we really think that there is no-one outside prison who can give the necessary support to a vulnerable young mother?

The number of frontline operational prison staff was cut by 26% during the years 2010–2017. More than one in seven of employed officers left the service last year. Staff retention remains a problem—Nearly half of officers who left the service last year had been in the role for less than three years, more than a quarter left after less than a year. Staff experience has declined as a consequence. They do not have the time or experience to look after new mothers and their babies.

These mothers need help and support outside the prison system. The Sure Start programmes introduced by Labour in 1998 were fantastic with the aim of *"giving children the best possible start in life"* through improvement of childcare, early education, health and family support, with an emphasis on outreach and community development. They then switched to Sure Start Children's Centres some of which became charities which were set up to support parents of young children and which can improve the mental health of mothers and the functioning of families. Two of the main provisions were for Family Support, including support and advice on parenting, information about services available in the area and access to specialist, targeted services; and Parental Outreach and also Child and Family Health Services, such as antenatal and postnatal support, information and guidance on breastfeeding, health and nutrition, smoking cessation support, and speech and language therapy and other specialist support. Surely this is a brilliant and much better way to support young families and new mothers? But they had their funding cut when the coalition government took office in 2010. In February 2020, a report showed that 1300 centres closed during the last 10 years, meaning more than one in three Sure Start centres were axed under the Conservatives. Only today as I write (12th July 2024), Polly Toynbee of the *Guardian* urges the new government to restart them. Evidence and evaluations now show that those children who were near Sure Start Centres at the age of five are now doing better at GCSEs than their peers who lived too far away to be able to go to them.

But I repeat: no pregnant woman should be sent to prison. It signifies a failed state and an uncivilized and uncaring society.

We go back now, to the largest women's prison in the country. How is **Holloway** getting on? Are conditions more amenable to women's needs? Are there enough experienced staff? Are there fewer women and are there any pregnant women still there? Surely after the critical inspection by Sir David Ramsbotham things will be better.

Let's have a look. His last inspection was in **2000** and his successor was Anne Owers. Expecting to find some improvement in her inspection in **2002** she said it was still suffering from many of the problems identified two years ago, with parts of the jail infested with cockroaches and feral pigeons and *"severe deficits"* in the regime. She found that women were denied showers more than twice a week even if pregnant or had just given birth, phone contact with families was difficult, and staff shortages meant children's visiting days had been stopped. But worse than all of that she also found that there were 13 girls under the age of 18 being held there. Three of them were pregnant and likely to have their babies while they were inside.

She condemned the prison regime as being *"wholly inadequate"* and that *"Girls, and particularly sentenced girls, are not supposed to be held in Holloway, and indeed should not be. But they were there."*

So we move on to the report **in 2010** with a new Chief Inspector Nick Hardwick.

I begin with a little bit of good news. This involves educational courses. *"There were approximately 100 full-time places in education. Women were very positive about their involvement in education and all women were offered a three week taster programme designed to help develop personal learning programmes. The provision included social and life skills as well as basic skills."*

The report goes on to say that, *"Achievements in education were generally satisfactory when women were able to complete the course, but few women achieved formal English for speakers of other languages qualifications, mostly because of the short time they spent in the prison. The majority of teaching and learning was satisfactory, with some good features. There was some good distance learning work at higher level, including Open University, and women received support for their studies."*

However elsewhere in this report there is much criticism.

> *"Electricity was switched off during the day so women who remained in their rooms could not use fans, kettles and other equipment."*

> *"Mothers and their babies were still unreasonably confined to their rooms after 8pm. Not all women separated from their babies at birth or afterwards on units elsewhere in the prison had care plans."*

"An appropriately qualified manager for the mother and baby unit should be appointed with sole responsibility for the unit, which should include childcare professionals in its day-to-day management and operation."

And then there is this:-

"Almost 60% of women in our survey, significantly more than the comparator, said they had felt unsafe in the prison" and *"There were a high number of incidents of self-harm and it was to the credit of the prison that there had been no self-inflicted deaths since 2007 despite the very vulnerable population."*

So there you have it. The prison is given credit for its lack of suicides. This is the low bar given to women in prison.

The Chief Inspector concludes his report with the following words: *"Holloway remains an extremely difficult prison to run safely and effectively. The efforts of managers and staff had succeeded in maintaining progress in most areas, though not all. They were, however, hampered by two things. One is the unsafe and unsatisfactory design of the prison. The other, as the Inspectorate has repeatedly pointed out, is the lack of strategic direction and effective operational management within the women's prison system in general, so that there is little informed operational support for Holloway's difficult and multi-layered role. Unless both are confronted and dealt with, Holloway will continue to drain its managers and struggle to meet the needs of the women it holds."*

And so it goes on with repeated critical reports year after year until we hear this. On the **15th November 2015** it was suddenly announced that HMP Holloway would be closed and the site sold off. This came as a huge shock to many, not least its 500 residents, who were left distressed about what this would mean for them.

In his 2015 Spending Review George Osbourne said that around 3,000 new homes will be created by redeveloping the old prison sites, as new prisons were being planned to replace Victorian jail 'relics'.

But I have just discovered that this prison, which was originally built for 700 male prisoners, was completely rebuilt on its 10 acre site, between **1971 and 1985** in a style designed to meet the perceived needs of women prisoners. And in 1977 a Mother and Baby Unit was added, which subsequently closed in September 2013. I find it difficult to believe that this happened relatively recently and that the new design aimed for a more humane environment, with cells arranged along corridors instead of wings. The focus shifted toward rehabilitation, resembling a hospital rather than a traditional prison. However, it is said that *"the effectiveness of these changes remains a subject of debate."*

Exactly they do. We have seen the prison being described as totally unsuitable year after year but just 30 years later, after a complete rebuild, its format is still poor and unsuitable and a complete nightmare for all those working there or incarcerated there.

And here we have the then Justice Secretary Michael Gove in a written statement in **2015** saying Holloway's *"design and physical state"* did not provide the best environment for the rehabilitation of offenders. He described HMP Holloway as *"inadequate and antiquated"* and cited inspection reports that noted the *"size and poor design make it a very difficult establishment to run."* But it was supposed to be a new design. It was only 30 years old. So now it is to close permanently and this dreadful prison will be consigned to the history books. So what will happen to the women prisoners? Will they release those 500 women who will not cause a crime wave in London I wonder? Such a good opportunity to do so. Will they be treated wisely and compassionately?

Well I have to disappoint you because in **2016** when the prison finally closed these women were sent to prisons outside London so taking them miles away from their families, communities and support services. It became much more difficult to maintain family visits and connections to their children. Many had to give up the education courses they were doing and of course had to part from the staff who had been helping them. Of course they were not released in order to have support in the community. Referring to Holloway prison in **1986,** Dr. Dorothy Speed, their principal medical officer and a psychiatrist, produced a long paper about the psychological effects and treatment of women in Holloway and I pick out just one sentence when she says *"Confinement in so dreadful a place was actually a form of torture which could drive people mad."* And the torture goes on.

So what is happening to the Holloway site? This is what Andrew Neilson, Director of Campaigns at the Howard League for Penal Reform thinks.

He said that *"Holloway is earmarked for closure, and the inspectorate is entirely right to say that the fall in the number of women in prison presents an opportunity to reduce the number of prison places available for them. This report supports our view that money made from the sale of Holloway should be invested in providing smaller units and finding a way to maintain the good resettlement and support services currently available in Central London, which will be difficult to replicate if women are relocated to Downview. (A closed women's prison in Surrey.) We need to know more from the Ministry of Justice about its plans. Simply moving women from Holloway to Downview could create more problems than it solves."*

Downview Prison was originally a remand centre for young offenders, and it transitioned into a women's prison in 2001.

Unfortunately the government chose not to listen to Andrew Neilson or others and the site was eventually sold to the Not-for-profit Peabody Housing Association in 2019 who are planning to build nearly 1,000 homes of which 60% would be *"affordable"* housing. The building will be done in three stages and in the first stage there will be 429 new homes. They hope to welcome the first residents in 2027. As a nod to the history of the site they plan to open a Women's Building that will house support services tailored to the needs of women from the local community. They say that the new community facilities, training and job opportunities, and green spaces there will have huge benefits for the local community.

Peabody goes back a long way and was founded in 1862 by George Peabody, an American banker, philanthropist and social visionary.

On their web site they say that *"We opened our first estate in Spitalfields in 1864. Since then, we've grown to house more than 220,000 people. We continue to build on our pioneering history, adapting to the changing needs of Londoners with innovations in affordable, sustainable housing. Our aim remains to improve people's lives through better housing and a sense of community belonging."*

So it is taking a while and whilst it is not 3,000 new homes this is a good outcome for Holloway prison site. And these are the sort of people who improve the future chances of so many who are in need.

So this is another charity that works with disadvantaged people and does amazing things but as someone pointed out they are only there because of the failings of governments.

But for women, as with young people, in so many cases prison is really never the answer.

And for women **and** men serious mistakes can be made.

MISCARRIAGES OF JUSTICE

There have been many miscarriages of justice over the years but I will just mention three. These are cases in which I have taken a personal interest. Two are women and one is a man. Although all were legally acquitted, the result on their lives has been catastrophic and has caused permanent damage and in one case an early death.

The six most common factors which contribute to miscarriages of justice are:-

- Eyewitness misidentification
- Faulty forensic analysis
- False confessions by vulnerable suspects
- Perjury and lies stated by witnesses
- Misconduct by police, prosecutors, or judges
- Ineffective assistance of counsel.

In some cases you can find all six.

I will begin with the women.

If a mother is in prison accused of killing her baby she is there for one of two reasons. Either it is because she is suffering from chronic and severe post-natal depression having had insufficient emotional or practical support, or she is innocent and is suffering from a devastating and traumatic miscarriage of justice. The following women were in prison for killing their babies.

I begin with Sally Clark who was arrested in February 1998 and convicted in November 1999. I remember this case very clearly and became more and more horrified the more I read about it.

Sally Clark was a solicitor and was married to Steve Clark who was also a solicitor. They had married in 1990 and on 22nd September 1996 their first son Christopher was born. Sally had always been interested in law and after meeting Steve decided to switch from her career in Citibank to pursue the law career she had always wanted. This meant that they were a bit later than many of their friends in starting a family but they were both over-joyed at his birth. He was a healthy baby but Sally Clark suffered from post-natal depression. Just over two months later on 13th December Christopher was found unconscious in his cot and was declared dead after being transported to hospital. This was thought to be a case of 'sudden infant death syndrome' or SIDS as they like to shorten this to. To lose a baby in such circumstances is a trauma which is impossible to fully imagine. But Sally Clark had treatment for her depression and they were delighted to give birth to their second boy, Harry two years later on the 29th November 1997. He was three weeks premature but then the unimaginable happened. He was also found dead just eight weeks later. The grief is unimaginable.

And then this. A month later Sally and Steve were arrested for murder. The charge against Steve was quickly dropped, presumably because on both occasions he had been away and Sally had been in the house alone. So she was tried for the murder of her two sons.

This poor woman was later found to have been completely innocent so for this to happen to her is beyond belief. It has been described as, *"without doubt, one of the most hideous and hellish miscarriages of justice of our times."*

She always denied the charge but was in prison for three years where she was vilified for being a child killer. Some of her fellow inmates did come to believe in her innocence but until that time she was spat on and sworn at and treated abominably.

Throughout the entire proceedings she was supported by her husband and he eventually discovered some vital information which helped to prove her innocence.

The prosecution case was led by Robin Spencer QC, and was controversial from the start for its involvement of the paediatrician professor Sir Roy Meadow, who was former professor of paediatrics at the University of Leeds. He testified at Clark's trial that the chance of two children from an affluent family suffering cot death was 1 in 73 million. He likened the probability to the chances of backing an 80–1 outsider in the Grand National four years running, and winning each time.

Well if you look back to my words about these two deaths I did say it seemed unbelievable.

But the first trial was widely criticised for the misrepresentation of statistical evidence, particularly by Meadow. He went on to state in evidence as an expert witness that *"one sudden infant death in a family is a tragedy, two is suspicious and three is murder unless proven otherwise"* (Meadow's law).

Meadow's calculation was based on the assumption that two SIDS deaths in the same family are independent.

But this argument was destroyed by Professor of Mathematics Ray Hill of Salford University. He said that *"there may well be unknown genetic or environmental factors that predispose families to SIDS, so that a second case within the family becomes much more likely than would be a case in another, apparently similar, family."*

He said that *"When a cot death mother is accused of murder, the prosecution sometimes employs a tactic such as the following. If the parents are affluent, in a stable relationship and non-smoking, the prosecution will claim that the chances of the death being natural are greatly reduced, and by implication that the chances of the death being homicide are greatly increased. But this implication is totally false, because the very same factors which make a family low risk for cot death also make it low risk for murder."*

He concluded that *"after a first cot death the chances of a second become greatly increased"* by a dependency factor of between 5 and 10.

Although double SIDS is very rare, double infant murder is likely to be rarer still, so the probability of Clark's innocence was quite high. Hill calculated the odds ratio for double SIDS to double homicide at between 4.5:1 and 9:1. Hill also said that Meadow *"conveniently ignored factors such as both the Clark babies being boys – which make cot death more likely".*

But also for some inexplicable reason the pathologist Dr. Alan Williams withheld the results of bacteriology tests on Clark's second baby which showed the presence of the bacterium *Staphylococcus aureus* in multiple sites including his cerebro-spinal fluid. During the trial the jury asked specifically if there were any 'blood' test results for this child. Williams returned to the witness box to deal with their query. He was specifically asked about an entry in the notes referring to 'C&S' results. These referred to samples taken for culture and sensitivity (bacteriology) tests. In his responses, he failed to reveal the existence of these withheld test results.

But later, it came to light that microbiological tests showed that Harry had a colonisation of *Staphylococcus aureus* bacteria, which indicated that he **had** died from natural causes, but the evidence had not been disclosed to the defence. It was discovered that this evidence had been known to the prosecution's pathologist, Alan Williams, since February 1998, but was not shared with other medical witnesses, police or lawyers.

Why on earth would he do this?

It was due entirely to her husband that this was discovered.

Every evening he worked on her case, consulting experts and building up a file of more than 2,000 documents on his computer. In February 2002, Macclesfield Hospital, under pressure from Marilyn Stowe, a Leeds-based solicitor who had provided her services free of charge to Steve and Sally because she felt that *"something was not right about the case"*, finally released the medical notes on both Christopher and Harry.

Steve spent every evening working his way through them assiduously. Among the hundreds of pages was the microbiology report that freed his wife.

"I almost threw it away — except, by then, I'd learnt that you don't throw away anything," he says. *"It looked like a blood test, and I thought, 'Surely everybody has seen this'. But then I remembered Williams saying at the trial that there hadn't been any blood tests on Harry."*

In fact, the report contained the results of swab tests — sent to Williams but never presented at Sally's trial — which established that at the time of his death Harry's stomach, lungs and spinal fluid were riddled with *Staphylococcus aureus* bacteria, an early form of meningitis. Professor James Morris, consultant pathologist at Lancaster Royal Infirmary and an expert in sudden infant death syndrome and bacteria, was asked by Sally's legal team to look at the report. His conclusion was unequivocal. *"Harry died of natural causes: an overwhelming staphylococcal infection; no other cause of death is sustainable."* Ten other specialists confirmed his view.

I actually remember reading this at the time and feeling completely overwhelmed and amazed at the tenacity of Sally's husband.

It also became clearer that the statistical evidence presented at Clark's trial was seriously flawed.

For her second appeal a report regarding the medical evidence was provided by Sam Gulino, a prosecution forensic pathologist for the State of Florida, US. He commented scathingly about the poor quality of the pathologists' work in these cases: *"Throughout my review, I was horrified by the shoddy fashion in which these cases were evaluated. It was clear that sound medical principles were abandoned in favour of over-simplification, over-interpretation, exclusion of relevant data and, in several instances, the imagining of non-existent findings."*

So in January 2003 the conviction was overturned and Sally Clark walked free.

Journalist Geoffrey Wansell called Clark's experience *"one of the great miscarriages of justice in modern British legal history."* As a result of her case, the Attorney General, Lord Goldsmith, ordered a review of hundreds of other cases. Because of this two other women convicted of murdering their children, Donna Anthony and Angela Cannings, had their convictions overturned and were released from prison and Trupti Patel, who was also accused of murdering her three children, was acquitted in June 2003. In each case, Roy Meadow had testified about the unlikelihood of multiple cot deaths in a single family.

Sally Clark had been suspended from the Roll of Solicitors in 2001 after her murder conviction and I remember being very concerned about this so I was delighted to hear that she was told in February 2003 she could practise law again after the conviction had been quashed.

And I was delighted to hear that Professor Roy Meadow was struck off the medical register by the General Medical Council in 2005 for serious professional misconduct. And in June 2005, Alan Williams, the Home Office pathologist who conducted the postmortem examinations on both the Clark babies, was banned from Home Office pathology work and coroners' cases for three years after the General Medical Council found him too guilty of *"serious professional misconduct"* in the Clark case.

But of course no-one comes out of an experience like this unscathed. I remember seeing Sally Clark as she walked out of prison and I was shocked by her appearance. Expecting to be really excited for her I was horrified. She was very thin and looked worn-out and as she said *"There are no winners here. We have all lost out."*

She did not in fact return to work but became a full-time mother as she had had a third boy during her trial and she wanted to give him her full attention. However in September 2005, she began proceedings against the pathologist who carried out the post-mortems on her two sons. She used the 17th Century law of Misfeasance in Public Office to make a High Court claim for damages. Her representatives said she was forced into this because she had never been fully reimbursed for her legal costs. We hear this so many times. The difficulty people have in getting any sort of financial compensation not just for legal costs but for loss of earnings, for mental and emotional distress, and for ongoing ill-health. I think we need to take look at this law.

The tort can be traced back to 1703 and was revived in 1985 so it is a very old law that has been increasingly used in recent years. The legal definition states that *"Misfeasance is a term in Tort Law that describes an act that is legal but performed improperly, causing harm to another party."*

The amount of compensation she received has never been publicly disclosed and there is some debate about whether or not she received any but she never recovered from this ordeal. Steve gave an interview to Catherine O'Brien of *The Times* in June 2004 in which he said that *"According to the psychiatrist who has assessed Sally, she is suffering from an "enduring personality change" caused by a "catastrophic experience".* Essentially, Steve says, it means *"that she is not the happy, confident person she was before this happened to her. She is vulnerable, she has panic attacks, she gets flustered by things that most of us just deal with. She constantly feels that people are judging her and it is a vicious circle."*

On the 15th March 2007 Sally Clark died alone at her home at the age of 42. There were various causes of death cited but I believe that it is obvious beyond all reasonable doubt that she died of a broken heart. She never got over the deaths of her two baby boys and the experience of being wrongly convicted and spending three years in prison was more than anyone could be expected to cope with.

Then in November 1999, the very month when Sally Clark was being convicted for the murder of her two babies, another young mother was about to be wrongly arrested for the murder of her two sons. This was Angela Cannings. She was charged with the murder of her seven-week-old son, Jason, who died in 1991, and of her 18-week-old son Matthew, who died in 1999. She had already suffered when her first child, Gemma, died of Sudden Infant Death Syndrome (SIDS) in 1989 at the age of 13 weeks, although she was never charged in connection with Gemma's death.

So she goes to court and we hear from many expert medical people. A Dr. Christine Scott, a Salisbury pathologist, had already concluded that both Gemma and Jason had died of sudden infant death syndrome and we also hear that another eminent paediatric pathologist Professor Emery had revised her original findings after revisiting the Cannings and agreed with Dr. Scott.

But a Professor Berry took the stand and gave some very disturbing evidence. He was a retired consultant from Bristol who had carried out the post mortem on Matthew as well as reviewing those on Jason and Gemma. He told the court that he had found evidence of bleeding in Jason's lungs in the form of siderophages. Apparently there are many natural reasons why they could be present but he said that in Jason's case here was no natural reason apparent. He was suggesting smothering.

And then once again we see the name Professor Sir Roy Meadow, who also accused her of smothering her two children. When he gave evidence in this trial the results of the Sally Clark appeal was not yet known and therefore the jury proceeded on the basis that he was an expert witness of great distinction, if not pre-eminence in his field. He had been knighted and had been awarded the Donald Paterson prize of the British Paediatric Association in 1968 for a study of the effects on parents of having a child in hospital. So he was very respected by everyone in his field of medicine.

His evidence of his testimony showed once again that there was absolutely no doubt in his mind that the three babies had been smothered by their mother who each time was alone in the house with them. Which is of course so often the case with babies. Mother at home whilst father goes to work. He had never met with Angela Cannings or spoken to anyone who knew her such as her GP or health visitors but this is a small part of what he said in court: *"I don't find a likely diagnosis of a naturally known condition. One then goes on to say, well, it is possible it is a condition that is not yet understood by doctors or described by them?—and that must always be a possibility. But nevertheless as a doctor of children I'm saying these features are those of smothering."*

Then a consultant paediatrician, Dr. Ward Platt from Newcastle, gave a similar view. He actually dismissed the idea of any possible genetic cause of these deaths saying that what had happened in her Irish family was too genetically distant. Before the trial the Cannings had looked into her Irish family and discovered that her second cousin had had seven children. Two had died of cot death, a baby boy had had to be resuscitated when he stopped breathing, a baby girl had had to be treated with caffeine for nine months because of concerns at how deeply she was sleeping and two others also had problems.

His whole manner in court was extremely aggressive and by now three eminent medical people had decided that without doubt smothering was the cause of the deaths of these three children.

Her defence counsel was the eminent barrister Mr. Michael Mansfield QC whom she found to be very human and very concerned about the effect all of his was having on her and her family. Of course the court listened to many family members and friends giving glowing references as a good mother but on Tuesday April 16th 2002 the jury found her guilty of the murders of Jason and Matthew.

The judge in this case was Judge Heather Hallett and when the verdict came through she hit out at the *"classic kind of injustice"* of mandatory sentencing that forced her to impose a life sentence. Her words as she sentenced her to life imprisonment were quite extraordinary and need repeating here.

"There was no medical evidence before the court that suggested there was anything wrong with you when you killed your children. I have no doubt that for a woman like you to have committed these terrible acts of suffocating your own babies there must have been something seriously wrong with you. All the evidence indicates that you wanted the children and apart from these terrible incidents you cherished them. So in my layman's view, it is no coincidence that these events took place within weeks of your giving birth. It can, in my view, be the only explanation for why someone like you could have committed these acts when you have such a loving and supportive family."

So in effect she is saying that she must have been suffering from post- natal depression. She also said that, *"It's not my decision when you will be released, but I intend to make it known in my remarks that, in my own view, you will never be a threat to anyone in the future."*

These are really strong words from a highly respected judge and caused a sensation amongst the legal profession at the time. So as I say at the beginning of this chapter if a mother is in prison for murdering her babies she is either suffering from post-natal depression or is innocent.

With the benefit of hindsight of course we know that Angela Cannnings was innocent.

So how was this proved?

On the 11th June 2003 some news came bursting through the prison where Cannings had been for over a year. Yet another mother, Trupti Patel, who had been accused of murdering her two boys and a girl had been acquitted.

"She's free, she's out, she's not guilty Ange" one of the lifers shouted. *"She's just like you and they said not guilty."* Someone else said *"You're walking Ange. You're walking. You're out of here."*

Cannings had been following this trial for a month by then and she had been devastated to learn that Patel had the same prosecuting counsel as she had had and ......here we go again,....... Roy Meadows as a key witness. *"In general"* he had said *"an unexpected death does not run in families."*

But a week later Trupti's grandmother had told the court that she had lost five of her twelve children in infancy. She was eighty years old and had flown in from India and through an interpreter was asked in court if she knew what had killed her children. *"No"* she said. *"This is something God takes care of. We leave it to God."*

It took the jury just ninety minutes to deliver a unanimous not guilty verdict.

"It's a matter of time, Ange" her friend in prison said. *"Just a matter of time."*

By this time too, Sally Clark's sentence had been quashed and gradually Cannings noted a change in the attitude of the girls on her wing. They started to treat her differently and became friendlier and she felt able to relax a bit although never allowing herself to think about the possibility of freedom for herself.

John Sweeney, an investigative journalist who worked for the BBC was making a documentary about this case and so was able to get sufficient funding to travel to Ireland in order to research the Canning's family history. He found some very important information. There had been more cot deaths in her immediate family. Her great grand-mother had lost a baby and her grand-mother had lost two children. They also discovered that her father had had a secret liaison some years previously and she had a half-sister and one of her children had suffered similar problems to those of Angela's. So there had been eight cot deaths in four generations of her family.

At her appeal a medical expert from the London School of Tropical Medicine, Professor Robert Carpenter, who had reviewed the latest information on cot deaths said that he believed the chances of her smothering her children and leaving no telltale signs were just 5%. He was about to publish new research which showed that children who suffered breathing attacks were ten times more likely to suffer cot deaths. He also condemned Professor Meadow's interpretation of the statistics about the likelihood of three children in the same family dying of cot death as a 'travesty'.

Lord Justice Judge addressed the court and concluded his remarks by saying *"These convictions are unsafe and accordingly they will be quashed and Mrs. Cannings will be discharged."*

After 18 months in prison, on the 10th December 2003, she walked out of prison a free and innocent woman.

But of course, as we have seen, no-one goes through this sort of trauma and emerges unscathed.

Angela already had a daughter, Jade, who had been four years old when her mother was first arrested. Her first task therefore was to bond with her daughter, now eight, who had found it difficult to understand why her mother had been absent from her life. She had been well looked after by her father and had become very close and reliant on him. The other thing Angela did was to write a book about her experience called *"Against All Odds"*. I bought this book just after it was published in 2006.

I read about how hard she tried to restore her life to some sort of normality and how hard she tried to restore her relationship with her husband and her daughter. By the end of the book things were looking good. She had also been awarded financial compensation. However the trauma proved too much for everyone and Angela and her husband Terry divorced and Angela has since remarried. Her daughter lived with her father and is now grown-up and married herself with a baby. She is estranged from her mother and does not allow her to see her grand-child.

The trauma goes on.

I now turn to a man who obviously did not lose any babies but lost twenty years of his life through wrongful conviction. There are in fact many innocent people in prison today and in a freedom of information request by the University of Law in 2020 they found that there were 1,336 successful appeals against both decisions of Magistrates' courts and the Court of Appeal between June 2019 and March 2020. The highest number of appeals against magistrates' verdicts was in London.

But I talk about the case involving Andrew Malkinson because it is such a recent high-profile case as it was only June last year (2023) that his conviction was finally quashed.

His case was the subject of a BBC Two programme *"The Wrong Man: 17 Years Behind Bars,"* which aired on 6 June 2024 when the case was thoroughly documented and which made shocking viewing.

It seemed to everyone watching this programme, and certainly to Andrew Malkinson, that the police were deliberately trying to cover up evidence in order in try to convict someone as soon as they could. It was a very high profile case. A young woman had been assaulted, strangled until unconscious and then raped as she was walking home one evening. *"He's got to be caught"* said Greater Manchester Police, *"or he'll do it again."* So this was the charge against Malkinson: rape and attempted murder.

On 2nd August 2003, in the early hours of the morning, police knocked on his door, arrested him, hand-cuffed him and took him to the police station. At all times he protested his innocence. They took his DNA and he was so relieved because he knew that that would prove that any DNA found on the victim would not be a match with his. But they had an identity parade at 1 in the morning and the victim picked him as the man who had raped her. 100% sure she said. So he was remanded in custody awaiting trial. The trial began in February 2004 and he could not understand why there was no DNA given in evidence. They had the torn and ripped clothes of the victim so there must have been loads of DNA available.

Then there were two witnesses who said they clearly remembered seeing him on the day of the crime 6 months ago.

So the jury convicted him, with a majority vote 10-2 and he started his life sentence on 30th March 2004 for a crime he didn't commit.

We discover that Andrew Malkinson had been a good-looking young man who had always had his nose in a book, was very academic and he loved travelling. When arrested he was a 37 year old security guard in Salford, but it was his good brain and his good friends which helped him to prove his innocence. As I have said however, it took twenty years.

On his first day in prison he lodged an appeal. In July 2006 the appeal was dismissed saying there was not enough evidence to proceed.

But in February 2007 there was a review of some criminal cases and it was found that DNA evidence in so many of them had not been investigated properly and had often been contaminated.

Then a real breakthrough. Another man's DNA had been found on the victim's clothes. Malkinson was so relieved because at last he thought, his innocence would be proved. So the CCRC was asked to refer his case back to court.

We need to look closely at the CCRC. This is the Criminal Cases Review Commission and they are the only body which can refer cases back to courts for a fresh appeal. Their services are free and they are independent of the police, courts and the government. They have special legal powers to look into criminal cases and anyone can apply who believes they have been wrongly convicted or sentenced, including those who have previously lost an appeal.

But the CCRC decided that his case was still not strong enough and rejected this request.

After you have served your minimum sentence you are eligible to be considered for parole. But in order to be granted parole you have to acknowledge your crime and go on courses to help you to turn your life around. But of course Malkinson had committed no crime so he was unable to do this. *"Do you want me to lie?"* he asked them. Well of course they said no but added that if he didn't fully confess he would be incarcerated for ever. They told him he was in denial.

He was devastated. As he said *"Prison is such a dangerous place."* He said that there had been a murder in his prison and that people could approach you with hidden razors and other sharp instruments and you had to be aware all the time.

So in 2017 he wrote to a friend of his whom he had met when travelling in Holland. They had become very good friends and for a couple of years they had been a couple. We heard her speaking on the BBC programme and she said that although they had broken up they had remained really good friends.

She was amazing and wanted to do all she could to help as she knew he was innocent of such a despicable crime. She found a charity called 'Appeal.'

On their home website this amazing charity says:-

> "APPEAL is a charity and law practice dedicated to challenging wrongful convictions and promoting a fairer justice system. We provide expert holistic assistance for individuals, and their families, who have experienced a miscarriage of justice and who cannot afford to pay for an appeal lawyer. We take wrongful convictions and unfair sentences to the Court of Appeal and the Criminal Cases Review Commission. We campaign on the wider issues our cases touch upon in order to achieve reform of the criminal justice system. We deploy our expert knowledge to identify particular issues of concern, conduct research and publish our findings."

In May 2017 they took on his case.

They wrote to the CPS, to the Greater Manchester Police and to the CCRC. They found that although DNA had been found in 2007 the CCRC had not conducted any interviews, not obtained any police files or looked at new DNA. When they insisted on seeing all available evidence, such as the torn and ripped clothes of the victim, they discovered that it had all been destroyed. But the Code of Practice issued under the Criminal Procedure and Investigations Act 1996 (CPIA) (section 23(1) provides clear guidance with a uniform direction that all material and objects should be kept until the prisoner is released from custody. So they were shocked when they realised it had been destroyed. But they then had a break-through when they discovered that an independent body, the Forensic Science Service in Birmingham, in a procedure known as Operation Cube, had actually kept tiny samples of the victim's clothes and had found a different DNA. This would have been known about in 2009.

So once again in 2012 they asked the CCRC to refer the case and in 2013 the CCRC once again said no it was still not a strong enough case.

We hear that at no time did the CCRC case manager read important evidence papers.

However by this time Malkinson had been working in prison doing a basic maths course and, by keeping his head down, the parole board eventually decided he was safe to be released and so he left prison in December 2020.

But he was not a free man. He was out on licence which meant that he was under tight supervision indefinitely.

APPEAL was not stopping here. They continued to dig and delve into his case and decided that it might be worth checking on those two witnesses. Well one of them had since died but they weren't going to let that stop them. They travelled to his home town and interviewed his friends. They discovered he had been on the Jeremy Vine show when he had admitted to being a heroin addict for 20 years. They found that both witnesses were known to the police as they had 26 convictions between them. When arrested, their charges were later withdrawn and they were let off with very lenient fines. The jury had not known any of this.

The victim too had described Malkinson inaccurately. She had described the attacker as being 3 inches shorter than Malkinson, with a hairless chest and no tattoos. Malkinson had chest hair and prominent tattoos on his forearms. She also said the attacker would have a "deep scratch" to his face. But Malkinson was seen at work the next day with no scratch to his face. This has never been properly explained.

So in 2023 the case went to the CCRC once more and this time they decided to refer the case back to the courts. There was much jubilation all round as I am sure you can imagine.

His conviction was eventually quashed on July 26th 2023 after yet another appalling miscarriage of justice. But of course so much damage had already been done. His mental health is not good and he finds it difficult to cope with things which caused him no problem before his imprisonment. He is getting a lot of support from friends, family and APPEAL.

But rightly so we hear that the Government ordered a judge-led inquiry, with the Justice Secretary (Alex Chalk) saying: *"Andrew Malkinson suffered an atrocious miscarriage of justice and he deserves thorough and honest answers as to how and why it took so long to uncover."* This inquiry could take a year to conclude.

A watchdog is also looking into Greater Manchester Police, which was deemed to have withheld evidence.

Through APPEAL Andrew Malkinson said *"The CCRC's delay in apologising to me added significantly to the mental turmoil I am experiencing as I continue to fight for accountability for what was done to me. The CCRC's failings caused me a world of pain. Even the police apologized straight away."*

At the time of writing (July 2024) he has had no compensation and is living on benefits.

Yet the Criminal justice Act of 1988 states that *"when a person has been convicted of a criminal offence and when subsequently his conviction has been reversed or he has been pardoned on the ground that a new or newly discovered fact shows beyond reasonable doubt that there has been a miscarriage of justice, the Secretary of State shall pay compensation for the miscarriage of justice to the person who has suffered punishment as a result of such conviction or, if he is dead, to his personal representatives, unless the non-disclosure of the unknown fact was wholly or partly attributable to the person convicted."*

Then today we hear this.

18th July 2024

Wonderful news! The independent report by Chris Henley KC is published today and the new Justice Secretary, Shabana Mahmood, is to seek the sacking of the chair of the CCRC. She said that Helen Pitcher was *"unable to fulfil her duties"* as chair of the CCRC. This damning report states that Malkinson could have been freed five years after receiving a life sentence. They conclude by saying that the CCRC's investigators and leaders failed to follow up evidence of innocence right up to 2022.

At last someone is being held accountable for this grievous miscarriage of justice.

My face is wreathed in smiles but goodness knows how Mr. Malkinson is feeling. And surely this will mean that compensation is on its way.

19th July 2024

Oh hang on a minute. We know exactly how Mr. Malkinson is feeling because he gave an interview on the 'Today' programme on Radio 4 this morning. My word he was calm and dignified and articulate but at the same time very angry. It transpires that Helen Pitcher, boss of the CCRC, is refusing to leave her post. She is insisting that she is the best person for the £95,000 salaried job which she does as well as holding down some non-executive directorships. She was also appointed last year as chairwoman of the Judicial Appointments which implies a conflict of interest. She is said to spend two days a week on each of these roles with the rest of the time spent on her private sector roles. As Emily Bolton director of APPEAL said *"leading the body charged with identifying miscarriages of justice is too important to be a part-time job."* Mr. Malkinson had nothing but contempt for her. It transpired that the CCRC were minded to turn down the third request for a referral. She refused to be interviewed last year whilst there was an ongoing inquiry and she refused to be interviewed this morning because of *"personal reasons."* Because the CCRC is an independent body she can only resign or be removed from her post by the King, acting on the recommendations of a panel which will be convened.

Well we see you Ms. Pitcher. And we don't like what we see.

Meanwhile the compensation has still not come through and he is still living on benefits.

So these are just three miscarriages of justice and there are many, many more. This is just the tip of the iceberg. Prison, as Mr. Malkinson says, is a living nightmare and, as I say over and over again, many should not be there.

But just as I am about to send this book to print on 16th September 2024 I hear of another appalling miscarriage of justice. This is a man called Oliver Campbell. He was accused of murder in 1990 when he was 19 years old. He was in prison for 11 years and then out on licence until last week when his murder conviction was quashed. So he has lost 34 years of his life and this is one of the longest miscarriages of justice in British legal history. It is a long and complicated story and this is the first time I have heard of it but we hear again of witnesses being ignored, the jury not being given all the essential information and DNA evidence of being dismissed.

We also hear again of the dither and delay of the CCRC. The first appeal to them in 1999 was unsuccessful after two years of deliberation. A new application was put forward in 2020 which included new evidence from DR. Gisli Gudjonsson, who was an expert on false confessions. This is because Mr. Campbell had learning difficulties due to an accident at birth and initially when questioned by the police he had eventually felt under a lot of pressure to plead guilty. But even all the prison officers had said for years that he was absolutely not capable of committing this crime. This time the CCRC took two years to approve the appeal and a further two years to reach court. What an appalling record.

He now has to fight for compensation.

Mr. Campbell echoes the words of Andrew Malkinson when he says that he is just the tip of the iceberg. He says there are lots of others like him in prison. *"Getting a conviction overturned is like climbing Everest."*

And in the coming months and years, believe me, we will continue to hear about many more.

SENTENCING

Anyone who has had anything to do with the sentencing guidelines or sentencing recommendations will tell you that they are a mine-field of complex procedures which would be impossible for the layman to comprehend. Even for the experienced barrister and judge it can be difficult and confusing.

The Secret Barrister says in his (or her) book of the same name that *"To try to make sense of sentencing is to roam directionless in the expansive dumping ground of the criminal law."*

Even the government understands the complexities as in a paper called **A Smarter Approach to Sentencing [published in 2020]** it says that *"In 2014, the government agreed that the Law Commission should begin work on a major reform to address this – drafting a new Sentencing Code to bring together the sentencing procedural law that courts rely on, setting out the relevant sentencing provisions in a clear, simple and logical way, and repealing old or unnecessary provisions. We have passed paving legislation in the last year, and in March this year, (2020) the Law Commission's Sentencing Bill was introduced to Parliament."*

It goes on to say *"The law governing sentencing procedure is overly complicated and has suffered from piecemeal reform, making it difficult for practitioners to follow and for the public to understand. Courts are spending time revisiting sentences and hearing appeals, or working out what law applies. This reflects badly on our justice system, it wastes time and money, and means victims are left waiting longer for resolution."*

So this has taken six years for this to see the light of day.

No one can accuse the government of having any sense of urgency whatsoever.

So there is no way in which I can explain any of it in detail. All I can do is explain some of the consequences. If you want the detail I recommend that you read the chapter in *"The Secret Barrister"* called 'The Big Sentencing Con.'

So what are the basic official purposes of sentencing? They are set out by the Sentencing Act 2020 criminal justice system as follows:

a) The punishment of offenders
b) The reduction of crime (including its reduction by deterrence)
c) The reform and rehabilitation of offenders
d) The protection of the public
e) The making of reparation by offenders to persons affected by their offence

It is obvious that, apart from the first one, none of these targets are being met.

There are many different types of sentences and many different guidelines for judges to consider but as our prisons are so full maybe it is further reason for some reform of these guidelines. It could be that sentencing is the key to reducing the prison population.

The main types of sentencing in the UK are custodial sentences, suspended sentences, community orders, fines and discharges.

As the new Justice Secretary says, prison will have run out of spaces within weeks. She has just announced that prisoners on standard determinate sentences will be released after serving 40% of their sentence rather than 50%. There will be exemptions for sexual and serious violent offenders. She said she had been left with no choice due to the fact that the last government had *"left this country on the brink of disaster"* with prisons *"on the point of collapse."* She continues to criticise the government led by Rishi Sunak and says they *"put their political careers ahead of safety and security of our country."* She concludes *"It was the most disgraceful dereliction of duty I have ever known. The last government left us with a time bomb."*

Then I see a bulletin from the Ministry of Justice published in **2021**, which *"presents prison population projections for England and Wales from July 2021 to March 2026. It is produced to aid policy development, capacity planning and resource allocation within the Ministry of Justice and Her Majesty's Prison and Probation Service (HMPPS)."*

The very first paragraph says *"The prison population is projected to increase to 98,500 by March 2026. This is largely a result of the recruitment of an extra 23,400 police officers, which is likely to increase charge volumes and therefore increase the future prison population."*

But as we have seen there is only capacity for 88,782.

So who has taken note of this prediction? Who has been planning for it? Err where will they go? Do they know the figures? Really worrying. And today (**19th July 2024**) we see that five members of the protest group 'Just Stop Oil' have been arrested and given custodial sentences of four, and in one case, five years. So many questions being asked. What is going on? Where will they go? Why is this so disproportionate? Is this because of the draconian bill called the Police, Crime, Sentencing and Courts Act, passed by the previous government, which was seen by many as an attack on human rights?

Indeed these particular protestors caused much distress by blocking the M25 for hours on end resulting in people missing funerals, hospital appointments and a myriad of other distressing situations but prison is not necessarily the right option in an overcrowded and expensive system and this action just endorses the urgent need for sentencing reform. I don't expect everyone to agree with me on this but in fact I now see that more than 1,100 lawyers, academics, artists and celebrities have called for an urgent meeting with the attorney general to address the *"injustice"* of these sentences. They say that *"With prisons at breaking point- how can these sentences be seen as anything other than insanity?"*

So many people have the wrong idea of what prison is. If they hear that certain prisoners are playing table tennis, or receiving books, or watching television they shout out that it is like a holiday camp. They seem unable to understand that the punishment is the deprivation of liberty. There is no greater punishment than that. And of course if prison reduced crime our prisons would be empty. But nearly 30% of all prisoners re-offend and are given another custodial sentence within 12 months of their release. It is a revolving door.

The average cost of keeping a person in prison for one year is £46, 692 and it definitely does not produce a feeling of safety amongst the community. Criminals are mixing together in prisons and young offenders especially can learn more criminal behaviour whilst there. At some point they will be released into the community so sentencing should aim to keep as many people out of prison as it possibly can.

Sentencing is, I believe, the key because if custodial sentencing is reduced then, for the smaller number still in prison, they will have the conditions, funding and staff to be able to be fully rehabilitated with education classes, therapy sessions, drug withdrawal help and health support. They can then be released as positive members of the community with continued support rather than be turfed out back onto the slag heap of inhumanity and despair.

Pre-sentence Reports. But before any sentence can be given the judge usually has to see a pre-sentence report.

And I see that these pre-sentencing reports are being reviewed. So what are they and will this make a difference?

In most court cases where the defendant has been found guilty or is pleading guilty and the judge is considering a sentence, a pre-sentence report is required.

This is drawn up after an interview by the Probation Service in order to obtain a fuller and more well-balanced picture of who the defendant is (as opposed to focusing purely on the offence) before passing sentence. Apparently this interview takes about an hour so the facts need to be presented very quickly and coherently. This is in order to find out if there are more facts about their situation which need to be taken into consideration. It provides an impartial assessment of the defendant's back-ground which, however good the defence barrister was, might not have been heard by the jury.

The effect on mothers seems particularly hard.

In a report in **September 2019 by a House of Commons Committee entitled "The Right to Family Life: children whose mothers are in prison."** they talk about these pre-sentence reports. They state that although judges are required to consider primary caring responsibilities roughly 17,000 children each year are being harmed when their mothers are sent to prison. It appears to be partly, they say, because the court does not have the correct information about whether the defendant has children and what the impact of a custodial sentence will have on them. In other words no PSR.

But they seem to contradict themselves in the same paragraph. They say that *"Given the range of factors that judges must already take into account in sentencing, the existing case-in-law and guidance already provided to the judiciary, we do not believe that sentencers should be subject to a further explicit statutory obligation to consider the welfare of offender's children when sentencing."*

What? I would have thought this was one of the first things they should consider, but then they say *"However we do agree with the committee's conclusion that it is vital that high quality pre-sentence reports are made available to sentencers by the National Probation Service to support sentencing decisions in line with these frameworks."*

They say that they note *"that the number of PSRs recorded as a percentage of sentences has steadily declined since 2012."* And that this may mean that *"opportunities are missed to inform sentencers where a defendant is a primary carer and of the impacts of custody on the child."*

I just find that is such a lot of gobbledy-gook just to say *"for goodness sake this person is the primary carer of a young child, is not a threat to the public and so should not be given a custodial sentence."*

But then it is obvious that I am not a lawyer.

So let us now look at all the different sentences.

CUSTODIAL SENTENCING.

Short sentences

It might not surprise you to know that it has been said over and over again that short sentences of under 12 months is not the answer so surely they could start by abolishing those straight away.

Rory Stewart, when he was Prisons Minister in December **2018,** gave evidence to the Justice Committee about short prison sentences. He told the committee: *"The wrong kind of short sentence actually endangers the public because the wrong kind of short sentence increases the chance of reoffending. The wrong kind of short sentence destabilises a prison."*

He has also argued that short jail terms are only serving to increase crime by mixing minor offenders with hardened criminals.

David Gauke agreed with Rory Stewart. He was the Secretary of State for Justice at that time, and was the first Justice Secretary to advocate for the abolition of short sentences. We had high hopes of this happening but Rory Stewart was only in post for a year because he was stripped of the whip by Boris Johnson in 2019 and David Gauke also had the whip removed in 2019 because he refused to work under the leadership of Boris Johnson. This was at the time, you may remember, when we had 12 justice secretaries in 14 years.

In a speech in February **2019** David Gauke said: *"In the last five years, just over a quarter of a million custodial sentences have been given to offenders for six months or less; over 300,000 sentences were for 12 months or less. But nearly two-thirds of those offenders go on to commit a further crime within a year of being released."* He said *"Why would we spend taxpayers' money doing what we know doesn't work, and indeed, makes us less safe?"*

The Howard League was also urging ministers to bring forward legislation to make the change a reality and prevent more people being swept into crime and despair.

Frances Crook, former Chief Executive of the Howard League for Penal Reform, said: *"Ministers have rightly identified that we must ease pressure on the prison system, and abolishing short sentences would be a welcome first step."* She said that *"Further action to reduce the prison population would save lives, protect staff and prevent more people being swept into deeper currents of crime and despair."*

Nearly 60% of criminals given short sentences will commit at least one serious offence within the first year of release. There is no time to get onto any education programme in just six months and even twelve months is too short.

A **2010** study found nearly half of all short-term prisoners spent all day in their cells. Little was done to help them break their pattern of behaviour during or after their time in jail.

I then see a website called **UK Parliament's POSTbrief 52 titled 'The Use of Short Prison Sentences in England and Wales.'** This work is published to support Members of Parliament and was published on the 27th July **2023**.

I just note a few points. It reports that *"In **July 2019**, the UK Government announced plans to launch a public consultation and publish a Green Paper setting out proposals on this issue. However, this was never published.*

*"In **June 2021**, during the passage of the Police, Crime, Sentencing and Courts Act 2022, Shadow Minister for courts and sentencing Alex Cunningham tabled amendments related to short prison sentences for Parliamentary debate (See Hansard Police, Crime, Sentencing and Courts Bill (Eighteenth sitting)) , however these were not voted on or added to the Act."*

"They (short sentences) are often given for low level offences, repeat offences or punishment for non-compliance to suspended sentence requirements."

In 2022, 5% of the sentenced prison population in England and Wales was serving a short immediate custodial prison sentence of less than 12-months. There has been a growing consensus that short prison sentences have limited effectiveness in reducing reoffending, or in achieving other goals such as rehabilitation, compared to community orders and suspended sentence orders. They may also have wider undesirable impacts on the prison service and for offenders particularly for women and young offenders."

So there has been a growing consensus that short prison sentences have limited effectiveness in reducing reoffending or resulting in any rehabilitation, but there has been very little action which is no surprise to anyone.

There are dreadful stories of mothers being sentenced in court and she hears the words *"take her down"* without her having any time to make provision for her children's care. There is a chapter about children and prison in my book *"Our Lost Children"* where I talk about children being suddenly left on their own and it makes heart-breaking reading. There is a brilliant charity called 'Children Heard and Seen' (CHAS) which supports these children but there is no statutory government body, as yet, responsible for them.

As we have seen short sentences are enough for a mother to lose her children, her home, and her job. Is that really what we want?

So on the 5 December 2023 there is a **Sentencing Bill Fact Sheet: short sentences paper** from the Ministry of Justice.

In it they say that *"Our statistics show the shorter the prison sentence the more likely someone will go on to reoffend. More than half of offenders serving a sentence of less than 12 months go on to commit another crime. For those serving a sentence of six months or less it is 58%. Meanwhile, for offenders punished with Suspended Sentence Orders with requirements that are served in the community, the reoffending rate is 24%. The facts are clear – short prison sentences leave offenders stuck in a revolving door of re-offending."* And *"In the Sentencing Bill, the Government will legislate to introduce a duty on the courts to suspend short sentences of 12 months' custody or less."*

Well that, at last, is brilliant to hear.

And in the King's speech on the 7th November 2023 we hear that they will bring forward a bill which, amongst other things, will include a presumption that custodial sentences of 12 months or less be suspended.

Well I don't hear the word 'abolished' there but I suppose this is a start.

Oh no it isn't even that, as this law does not get passed due to the dissolution of parliament.

Long Sentences

It would appear that at the present time sentences are either too short or too long. We know that short sentences provide poor outcomes when community sentences would be more beneficial to everyone concerned, but judges are doling out longer and longer sentences for more serious crimes. So does this reduce crime I wonder?

Well I think I know the answer, which does sort of beg the question then why doesn't everyone? And then I hear well actually yes, a lot of people do know.

As the Secret Barrister says *"Prison as we presently do it is an expensive way of making bad people worse."*

Research for the Sentencing Council has shown that longer sentences do not effectively reduce crime. More than two in five adults (42%) are reconvicted of another offence within one year of release.

According to figures produced by the Prison Reform Trust we have a higher proportion of life sentenced prisoners than any other country in Europe including Russia and Turkey and the average prison sentence is much longer now than it was 25 years ago.

With prison sentences getting longer, more people are growing old behind bars. People aged 60 and over are the fastest growing age group in the prison estate. The number of people in prison aged 50 or over is projected to grow by around 1,000–2,400 people between 2022 and 2026 according to government estimates. To quote the Secret Barrister again he says that there is a moral cowardice amongst some politicians which prevents them from treating the public like adults. They like to say they are being tough about longer sentences but they don't want to pay for them so it is a complete waste of tax payers' money. It is costing nearly £47,000 to keep one person in prison for one year and they spend most of the time locked up in their cell having had with no rehabilitation whatsoever. Do they think we can't understand the futility of that?

The longer the sentence in an overcrowded prison the more difficult it is for the offender to restart their life once released.

And on September 6th 2024 a report is published by the Howard League in which five of the country's most senior retired judges call on ministers to *"reverse the trend of imposing ever longer sentences."* The report states that the UK is on the brink of *"US-style mass incarceration."*

They quote a paragraph from the Woolf Report which was written in 1991. *"Overcrowding has had a mesmeric effect on the prison system and has absorbed energy which could have been used in improving prisons. In addition, prisons are expensive and have damaging effects on prisoners. It is therefore important... to reduce the prison population to an unavoidable minimum."*

The report mentions all those whom I have written about here. Women, children, the mentally ill, the elderly and the illiterate and they say that *"Money spent on keeping more people in prison for longer is money wasted. Expenditure should be directed to reducing prison numbers by providing effective rehabilitation in prison and proper supervision and assistance to those who have served their sentences."*

They conclude *"We call for an honest conversation about what custodial sentences can and cannot achieve; their human and financial costs; and urge a return to more modest proportionate sentences across the board."*

IPPs (Imprisonment for Public Protection)

These are another example of ill-thought-out sentencing which has resulted in yet more over-crowding in our prisons. They were introduced in England and Wales in 2005 under the Criminal Justice Act 2003. These were indeterminate sentences for people considered *"dangerous"* but who did not merit a life sentence. So not necessarily in prison for a crime they have committed but for what they might do in the future. Basically they have to serve a minimum sentence but have no date for their release. Lord Clarke former justice secretary abolished these IPP cases in 2012 because they were seen to be unfair but it was not retrospective so there are still nearly 2,800 IPPs who have never been released and will still not know when they will be released. To quote just one example which was highlighted by Sky News is Thomas White who was handed a two year minimum prison sentence under IPP four months before the sentences were abolished, but remains in prison 12 years later.

The Howard League report states that *"the introduction by the last Labour government of the indeterminate sentence for public protection (IPP) exemplifies the dangers of poor sentencing policy. Abolished nearly 14 years ago, our friend the late Lord Brown described the IPP sentence as 'the greatest single stain on our criminal justice system'."*

In February 2024 the Centre for Crime and Justices Studies wrote a report about IPPs and suggested a five point plan to the government.

They called for them to: *"Release the most distressed prisoners on compassionate grounds. Launch a recovery and reparations programme for IPP prisoners. Ease restrictions for over-tariff IPP prisoners still in custody. Commit to review all forms of preventive detention. Complete a resentencing exercise for all those under an IPP as soon as possible."* Having had very little response from the Conservative government they then sign an open letter on July 11th 2024 to the new Labour government requesting action in their first 100 days. Their director Richard Garside says, *"In his first press conference as Prime Minister, last Saturday, Sir Keir Starmer described prisons as "broken". A practical first step in fixing the broken prison system would be for the government do what it promised to do in opposition: to "work at pace" to resolve the scandal of the IPP sentence. As well as freeing up much needed prison capacity it would finally draw a line under a dreadful sentence that has been a stain on our justice system for far too long."* The letter was also signed by UNGRIPP – United Group for Reform of IPP, IPP Committee in Action and JENGbA, The Howard League for Penal Reform, Prison Reform Trust as well as the Centre for

Crime and Justice Studies. The Prison Officers' Association and Napo, Amnesty, Inquest and Justice, those serving an IPP sentence and a number of academics, lawyers and experts in their field.

We wait to hear the response from the new prime minister.

Community Orders

We need to look at community sentencing to see if this is a good way to keep people out of prison whilst at the same time being a deterrent.

The Sentencing Council describes a community sentence as combining some form of punishment with activities carried out in the community. There are 13 possible requirements that offenders could be required to do and they can be given just one or a combination whatever seems appropriate.

They include 40 to 300 hours of unpaid work, house arrest, curfews, therapy such as anger management, treatment for alcohol or drugs, and a ban on travel. Electronic tagging might be applied. Community sentences are far less expensive than prison and for certain crimes are more effective in reducing re-offending. They help with rehabilitation as offenders are able to maintain family contacts and possibly employment contacts.

Because of all this it seems to me that it is a no-brainer to use community services wherever possible as it will also help with the present prison over-load.

But of course it is not always so straight-forward because these community sentences are controlled by the Probation Service and like everywhere else in the criminal justice system it is severely over-stretched.

In fact community sentences have been declining in recent years and although this could be because judges are giving more suspended prison sentences they feel it could also be because the Probation Service is struggling and it is important to discover why. If I mention just one name you might understand. **Chris Grayling.**

Here we go. Chris Grayling, when justice minister in **2014,** (disaster alert) contracted out the management of low-risk and medium risk offenders to private companies. This caused a great deal of worry as the 35 probation trusts in England and Wales previously running the sector were dismantled and it led to what was assessed as *"poor quality supervision"* of many offenders.

However by June **2021** there was a massive U-turn by the government and the probation service returned to public control. The system was deemed flawed and had cost the tax payer an extra £500 million.

But the service is struggling to meet demands. They are short-staffed and have workloads twice as large as their recommended capacity. A whistle-blower warned that risks to the public *"are significant"*.

In some cases staff had individual case-loads of more than 70 people.

So then we see a report by the outgoing Chief Inspector of Probation, Justin Russell in **2023,** who is calling for an independent review of whether the Probation Service should return to local control. I don't believe it.

He says that it has always been a locally delivered service and they need the freedom and flexibility to commit resources and staff to match local circumstances.

So there we have it. Prison sentences are failing and the Probation Service is failing which leads to community sentences failing.

And there seems to be no definite plan.

Oh no, wait a minute, I think this looks like a plan. It is a government response called:- **"Breaking the Cycle: Effective Punishment, Rehabilitation and Sentencing of Offenders"**

Just a fraction of what they say is *"The criminal justice system cannot remain an expensive way of giving the public a break from offenders, before they return to commit more crimes. We plan to transform the administration of punishment in this country to make it more robust and credible. Prisons will become places of hard work and industry, instead of enforced idleness."*

Well that sounds like a brilliant plan.

Oh wait a minute, I see that the date of this is December **2010.** But how about this one? This sounds really good. This is a Ministry of Justice consultation document entitled:-

"Punishment and Reform: Effective Community Sentences"

Again this is just a flavour of what it says.

> *"The Government has embarked on wholesale reform – beginning with prisons becoming places of meaningful work and training, not idleness, where many more prisoners will work a full working week, and the extension of payment by results, so that the taxpayer only funds rehabilitation services that work. Together with determined action in areas like mental health and addiction, these measures will help cut reoffending, protecting the public more effectively, whilst ensuring that wrong-doers are properly punished. The next stage of reform is sentences in the community and the operation of the Probation Service which supervises them. In two publications, on which we are consulting in parallel, I set out radical plans to make sentences in the community more credible and to reform probation so it is more effective in reducing crime, by extending competition and opening up the management of lower risk offenders to the innovation and energy of the widest possible range of providers."*

"We have published new Probation National Standards which provide more discretion on how probation services manage offenders, allowing more space for innovation."

Excellent so when was this published? Ah yes here it is. March **2012.** Well both of these were published under the Coalition government when Ken Clarke was Justice Secretary and these are excellent words and, who knows, if he had not been shuffled around in 2012 something concrete might have happened. But of course, as you know, what actually happened was that David Cameron, in a moment of intense aberration appointed Chris Grayling as Justice Secretary and the rest is chaos.

But off he went three years later in May **2015** and Michael Gove took his place.

So we then we go on to this year. In **February 2024** this is called **"Cutting Crime: Better Community Sentences. Response from the Ministry of Justice to the Justice and Home Affairs Committee."**

They write that *"The Ministry of Justice is committed to ensuring that community sentences offer a robust and rehabilitative alternative to custody, alongside other sentences such as suspended sentences with robust conditions attached. There is persuasive evidence that non-custodial sentences are, in certain circumstances, more effective than short custodial sentences in promoting rehabilitation, reducing reoffending, and driving down crime. Community sentences also deliver suitable and effective punishment for eligible offenders."* *"We are already working to improve the quality of community sentence delivery from the earliest stages of advice to court, through to the delivery of requirements and supervision."*

So there we have it. They all know the problems. They all know what is needed to rectify the problems. They have known for years and years but actually nothing was done.

Sentencing Guidelines

Then on April 1st 2024 we see new sentencing guidelines from the Sentencing Council which they say are now in force. Now, the Sentencing Council, produces guidelines on sentencing for the judiciary and criminal justice professionals and is responsible for the final decision as to what instructions go into these guidelines to sentencers. It is chaired by the Lord Chief Justice and has a majority of judicial members; guidelines are drawn up with reference to current patterns of sentencing and guideline judgements from the Court of Appeal. It is, therefore, an independent body with significant judicial input. Having looked at these guidelines, to an unprofessional eye, it looks as though everything is more complicated than ever, for I see an article in the BMJ on 3rd June this year (2024) which looks at some of the new mitigating factors which are being brought into force. They are particularly concerned with pregnant women which of course is one of my main concerns too. They talk about the 194 women spending time in prison while pregnant, and the 44 who gave birth whilst being held in custody.

"Thankfully," they say, *"in March this year, we saw a breakthrough. The Sentencing Council for England and Wales—the body responsible for the guidelines informing sentencing decisions—announced that pregnancy, birth, and the postnatal period will be included as a specific mitigating factor to be considered by magistrates and Crown Court judges."* Well I have to applaud this decision, at the same time as deploring the length of time it has taken to get here. The decision was based on research commissioned by the Sentencing Council and led by the University of Hertfordshire looking at equality and diversity in sentencing. And another brilliant charity also contributed to this research.

They are 'Birth Companions' who say on their web site that they are *"dedicated to tackling inequalities and disadvantage during pregnancy, birth and early motherhood. We were founded in 1996 to support pregnant women and new mothers in Holloway Prison. Since then we've become experts in meeting the needs of women living in the most challenging situations in prison and in the community."* The charities I come across as I write this book are inspirational.

This is indeed a huge, if long overdue, step forwards and the new mitigating factors took effect on **1st April 2024**.

However, (that word again), there was some disappointment. 'Birth Companion' said *"We had strongly urged the council to extend their definition of the postnatal period to cover two years after birth. This would have brought it in line with HM Prison and Probation Services' policy framework and with the period recognised by the government and many others as the "critical 1001 days" from conception to a child's second birthday. Although it is disappointing that the council limited the mitigating factor to 12 months postnatally, we hope that further training and support on fulfilling the needs of pregnant and postnatal women will ensure that sentencers take full account of the many risks and complexities associated with this period. Ending the use of prison for these women, be that sentences, remand, or recall, is the only way forward. This new mitigating factor sets us in the right direction—but more than guidance we need concrete policy and sentencing reform."*

To which I would add "and more common sense, humanity, compassion and support."

So in brief, they have amended mitigating factors around remorse, good character, steps taken to address addiction or offending behaviour, and age/maturity of defendant.

New mitigating factors are being applied to those with difficult or deprived backgrounds, which hopefully includes whether the defendant has been in care or not, what prospects they have regarding work or education, and the pregnancy one.

Then I see something for the Crown Court which concerns the offence of manslaughter. They have added strangulation, suffocation and asphyxiation as an aggravating factor to the loss of control and diminished responsibility guidelines and also they have incorporated coercive or controlling behaviour within the aggravating and mitigating factors relating to a history of violence or abuse.

This is long overdue because we hear of appalling cases whereby a woman (and it is usually a woman, but obviously will also apply to a man) is subjected to years of abuse, either physical or mental and emotional, by a bullying partner and then suddenly snaps and kills them.

But actually I say that, for goodness sake, all of these amended and new mitigating factors are long over-due.

So far as I can see they are all common sense, but as I do keep pointing out I am not a lawyer.

REHABILITATION IN

OUR PRISONS

We just need to be reminded now about the prisons and their general fitness to offer courses, education, therapy and a healthy and positive environment. So how is rehabilitation going?

Obviously in order to have positive and productive courses which will hopefully lead to employment on release there needs to be a safe, clean and healthy environment. Prison inspectors have been asking for this for years so surely, by now, in 2024 this should be the case.

We will look at the good news first.

HMP Liverpool is undergoing a multi-million pound refurbishment in which each of its wings is being renovated and brought into the 21st century on a rolling basis. The aim is to increase its current capacity of 840 prisoners by 350 to help tackle the nationwide overcrowding crisis. This should be achieved by 2025/26. The overhaul aims to provide lighter, airier living spaces with wardrobes, shelves for books, a TV and en-suite toilets. It is still a prison cell, though, so the windows will have ventilated grilles to combat drugs being smuggled in, and the shortage of prison places means offenders will still have to share cells with bunk beds.

And this is a brilliant idea.

Using new technology prisoners are given some autonomy over their lives through a computer system which, using their fingerprint, they can use to book gym, education and work sessions, request GP appointments, choose their meals from a menu, check their prison account balance and make general requests. The regime is designed to try to get prisoners back into the habit of work. Here, at last, we see some good rehabilitation going on. A bicycle workshop offers offenders the chance to repair bikes, including those donated by police as unclaimed stolen property. Once refitted, they are offered to charities. The prison's leather workshop has established links with the Liverpool satchel company to provide three prisoners with the training to become leather craftsmen, while the laundry is cleaning the overalls of staff at Slaters Workwear and mats for Golden Hygiene. One prisoner, six months from release, said: *"It is helping me back into the working environment. It makes me feel good and shows I am taking responsibility. I want to get back to work. I was a manager at Subway."*

So with the will and extra funding it can be done.

We need to find other examples.

Downview prison is a womens' prison and 10 years ago formed a partnership with the London College of fashion. They believe that this will reduce re-offending rates. The women here are training up to be machinists and are making jackets and skirts which look amazing. Many of them hope to get employment when released.

And at the prison's Clink Events kitchen, run by 'The Clink Charity', the women are able to prepare food for 490 people at London's Guildhall. This amazing charity works in 32 prisons training offenders. On their web-site they say that:-*"The prisoners at each of The Clink training projects train up to 40-hours a week whilst working towards gaining their City & Guilds National Vocational Qualifications. Simulating a professional working environment, prisoners with six to eighteen months of their sentence left to serve volunteer for the programme, going through full-time training in order to reach the required level to succeed in their respective industry"*

This is a wonderful way to reduce re-offending and to give often very vulnerable people a skill for life. It was great to see the Duchess of Cornwall, as she then was, visiting Downview in 2020 and talking to the women and taking a real interest in their work.

Rehabilitation courses in prison are essential if re-offending is to be reduced. As we have seen it is possible given the right conditions, enough staff, the will and appropriate funding.

Indeed the government continually places great importance on this. In **2016** we see a report by Dame Sally Coates called 'Unlocking Potential'. I just need to quote a couple of sentences when she says *"Let there be no doubt. Education should be at the heart of the prison system."* But although Sally Coates's report was publicly endorsed by the then justice secretary Michael Gove *"without hesitation"*, it has not been implemented in any meaningful way in the eight years since, as the parliamentary select committee on education noted in a **2022** follow-up.

Why, oh why, does this seem to be the recurring story with all prison reform ideas?

Then again in a '**Prisons Strategy White Paper published in December 2021** they set out a *"new plan to deliver the biggest prison building programme in more than 100 years creating the right prison conditions to reform and rehabilitate offenders and ultimately cutting crime and keeping streets safe."* This was under the Johnson administration.

And then in **September 2023,** under the Sunak government, they announce that *"Learning in jails is to be completely transformed through the introduction of a new Prisoner Education Service as part of a renewed push to skill up offenders and protect the public."*

Well better late than never I suppose. Why has no-one thought of this before in government I wonder? There are many charities which aim to help those in prison with literacy and numeracy skills and on-line courses but the government does not have a reputation for doing anything positive and we can actually remember a time when a Justice Secretary wanted to ban all books being sent to prisoners. Yes it was Chris Grayling who, in **2013**, issued an order to ban all small parcels containing books admitted into any prison. Oh my word the backlash was enormous. This is the land of Shakespeare, Milton, Keats, Dickens, Agatha Christie, Arthur Ransome, Enid Blyton, come on we all know the value of reading and although Grayling tried to defend this decision it was eventually overturned.

Frances Crook, of the Howard League, described the *"book banning"* policy as the *"most despicable and nastiest element of the new rules"*, adding it was part of an *"increasingly irrational punishment regime orchestrated by Chris Grayling"*. When the Howard League asked for a meeting with Chris Grayling he refused, calling the most renowned, respected and oldest prison reform charity in the world a *"small protest group."* The ignorance and stupidity is staggering. Which prime minister was irresponsible enough in a complete moment of aberration to make him Justice Secretary do you suppose? David Cameron.

Juliet Lyon, director of the Prison Reform Trust, said: *"Banning prisoners from receiving books in prison is just one of a number of mean and petty rules introduced by the justice secretary which add to the stress and strain of imprisonment while doing nothing to promote rehabilitation."*

A petition of authors reached almost 13,000 signatures and the charity 'Booktrust' said in a statement: *"Surely our efforts should be on encouraging more people in prison to read rather than punitive action to stop those that want to?"*

Prisons Minister Jeremy Wright, meanwhile, said a major reason restrictions were in place was to stop things like drugs being smuggled in.

I have news for you Mr. Wright. Our prisons are awash with drugs. They don't need to be smuggled in with books. Indeed many prisoners become drug addicts when in jail having not been addicts before.

Shadow justice secretary, Shabana Mahmood, said the policy was an example of *"the skewed priorities of a justice secretary who has no solutions to the problems in our prisons".* ,

So after a long campaign by the Howard League and others, in **December 2014** a judge declared the restrictions that were introduced by a new prison rule in **November 2013** *"unlawful".* By this time there was a new Justice Secretary by the name of Michael Gove. But Grayling had spent £72,000 of tax-payers money trying to defend it all.

But we return to **December 2023** when Charlie Taylor, Chief Inspector of Prisons, told the BBC that a *"fundamental reorientation"* of the prison system was the only way to reduce reoffending. In a report by Harrison Jones of BBC news he said that *"jails were failing to reduce the risk of prisoners reoffending, and that many inmates were failing to learn to read. Others",* he said, *"were taking part in courses which would not help them get jobs in future."* He also argued that the high availability of drugs in some prisons was hindering rehabilitation efforts, as he called for immediate action to give prisoners the skills they need for life in the workplace.

Overcrowding is a huge problem and Mr. Taylor believes there is not enough space for prisoners to be provided with the activities they need for suitable rehabilitation. It really is pretty basic common sense. If the prisons are over-flowing, and they are, then there is no room for anything else but containment. It is essential that there is a complete overhaul of the sentencing system so that far, far fewer people are sent to prison. Until that happens there will be very little progress.

But I think we now need to look closely at the recent reports of some of the most over-crowded prisons in order to fully understand these words by Charlie Taylor.

There has just been an escape from **Wandsworth** prison so we will start there.

On the **8th May 2024** there was an Urgent Notification about HMP Wandsworth by Charlie Taylor in a letter to Alex Chalk the then Justice Secretary. I quote a small part of what he said:-"*Overall rates of violence, including serious assaults, had increased since the last inspection and were higher than most similar prisons. In our survey, 69% of prisoners said they had felt unsafe at Wandsworth*".

"*There had been 10 self-inflicted deaths since the last inspection, seven of which had occurred in the last 12 months. The rate of self-harm was high and rising, and yet around 40% of emergency cell bells were not answered within five minutes.*" And then this:- "*A substantial lack of work and education spaces and poor use of those that were available meant there was very little purposeful activity. Most prisoners were unemployed and spent over 22 hours a day locked up.*" He also comments on the increasing availability of drugs and the poor standard of food. The Chief Executive at the Prison Reform Trust, Pia Sinha, branded the conditions there "*shameful*". She said: "*In my 24 years in the Prison Service, I'd say they're in the worst condition I've seen them.*" She says one of the aims of prison is rehabilitation but current conditions lead to "*trauma and re-traumatisation*" which will not "*help us to break the cycle*" and means inmates "*are going to come out of the other end in a worse state*".

We now visit **Pentonville** prison.

This is one of the oldest prisons in the UK having been built in 1842 and it has had no major structural improvements since then. A report by their Independent Monitoring Board published in **March 2023** found that it was "*unfit*" for inmates to live or to be rehabilitated due to a lack of privacy and erupting sewage.

Well yes, I think most of us would find learning difficult under those conditions.

Pentonville chairwoman, Alice Gotto, said it was *"disappointing"* the prison's population has continued to increase despite detailed evidence *"of the detrimental effect this would have on prisoners"*. There were now often two to a cell, and there were issues with water, heating and vermin, due to the prison's Victorian-era infrastructure. But a report by the HM Chief Inspector of Prisons on **11th–13th April 2023** did find some improvements which is encouraging to see with slightly improved staffing levels, although a high proportion of all prisoners still said that they felt unsafe. And the over-crowding continues. Originally designed to hold 520 people in single cells, it now has an operational capacity of 1,205, with two prisoners packed into each cell. The report says that *"Despite long-standing official National Statistics predictions for the increase in prison population, national leaders had failed to plan adequately for, and support the reduction of, the population at Pentonville. Instead, they intended to increase the population to 1,205 in the coming months, which would exacerbate the overcrowded and cramped conditions that many prisoners had to endure."* Then *"Attendance at off-wing purposeful activity remained low at about 60%."* But *"Access to education had improved."*

However, in September 2024 the BBC got access to Pentonville and once again I see shocking scenes of violence and chaos. There is shouting, screaming, metal doors banging, someone bleeding, people running, shoving and fighting and it reminds me of those scenes I saw at Feltham YOI all those years ago.

It would seem that the staff here are working hard to try to do their best in impossible circumstances but it is still a nightmare scenario.

Then we go to **Bedford.** HMP Bedford was put into special measures in **May 2018** after concerns over living conditions and violence levels. But by **2023** there had been no improvement. Charlie Taylor, and his team made an unannounced inspection in **November 2023.**

In this report he said *"Some of the accommodation in Bedford was the worst I have seen. On E wing, the smell of mould in one cell was overpowering, with the walls damp to the touch, while the underground segregation unit was a disgrace. Here, problems with the drainage mean that on very wet days, raw sewage covered the floor and the cells were dark, damp and dilapidated. Despite this, dedicated staff did their best to provide care for what were often very mentally unwell prisoners in wholly unsuitable conditions."*

And *"The provision of education was even worse than at our last inspection and was now poor. There were not enough places on offer, particularly in English and maths, where there were long waits to join courses. Attendance was much too low at just 52%."*

Also *"levels of violence remained very high, particularly assaults on staff which were among the highest in the country."*

But again the report says that staff were doing their best.

I find it extraordinary that anyone applies for a job in such prisons today.

Then I go to **Bristol** and see that the prison there was issued with an urgent notification in **2023**. One of the criticisms here was that men without in-cell toilets must call an officer to be escorted whenever they need to use the bathroom. *"Only 16% of prisoners in Bristol said cell bells were answered within five minutes, forcing them to use buckets and bins, which they empty out the window. The waste splashes into the cells below, causing an "overpowering" smell of urine,"* the inspector reported.

In response, the government committed to install in-cell toilets by **2025.** Goodness. No sense of urgency here then. And impossible to concentrate on any courses I would think with a full bladder.

Then I see a report on **HMP Lewes** prison and I pick out a few points which seem to apply to nearly every prison I look at. **HMP**

Lewes by HM Chief Inspector of Prisons 20–22 February 2023
"Priority concerns are:- "Staff shortfalls in many areas had slowed progress in achieving better outcomes for prisoners." "The most vulnerable prisoners were not sufficiently well cared for." "Areas of the prison were unacceptably dirty." "Time out of cell for prisoners was inadequate." "Violence at the prison was still too high and there was limited understanding of the causes and how to respond to them."

I could go on but then I see two reports which seem to cover the entire prison estate. **HM Chief Inspector of Prisons for England and Wales Annual Report 2022–23** printed on 5 July 2023.

> *"Despite final COVID-19 restrictions being lifted in May 2022, we found far too many prisons continuing to operate greatly reduced regimes in the last year. This meant that prisoners remained locked in their cells for long periods of time without the purposeful activity that would support a successful reintegration back into society at the end of their sentences. Over the last year I have consistently raised concerns with governors, the prison service and ministers that prisoners who have not had sufficient opportunities to become involved with education, training or work, and have spent their sentences languishing in their cells, are more likely to reoffend when they come out."*

And everyone who knows anything about the prison system will actually know this. Actually anyone with a functioning brain will know this.

Then in **May 2024** there is a report by openDemocracy which is an independent international media platform. On their website they say *"We produce high-quality journalism which challenges power, inspires change and builds leadership among groups underrepresented in the media."*

This is a much needed organisation in the UK just now.

Sian Norris who is their senior investigative reporter produced a prisoner survey data analysis which was published on the **6th May 2024.**

You will not be surprised to hear that it reveals *"widespread and systematic failings in safety, hygiene, healthcare, violence and release planning."*

She found that more than half of all inmates feel *"unsafe"* in 35 prisons.

And then I read a report in the media today (**24th July 2024**) about a group of people I never knew existed. They are called the National Tactical Response Group or 'Tornado Squads'. Basically this is a prison riot squad and they are struggling to cope with a huge increase in demand. They are, apparently, an *"elite team of officers"* who are trained to swoop into prisons when there is a dangerous, emergency situation usually involving violence and disorder. In last month alone they had to be deployed 75 times in prisons in England and Wales. When violence breaks out in many prisons at the same time they are completely over-stretched and are considering trying out *"more powerful weapons"* on prisoners. *"Small calibre impact launchers"* have been mentioned.

I am sure that many people reading this book will know all about these but I have to look them up as I have no idea what they are.

Oh my word. There is a whole market out there! Basically they are nasty but powerful projectiles which can cause severe damage without, hopefully, actually killing you.

There are roughly three categories: hard and forceful projectiles like rubber bullets fired out of guns which aren't really guns; chemical powders like pepper spray, and special technologies such as Tasers and *"weaponized sound waves."* I'm sure you will know what those are.

Yes well a policeman was stabbed in the chest at HMP Frankland prison in Durham this month on the **23rd July 2024** and obviously in emergency situations like this, drastic action is required. But really, with the ever-rising violence in our prisons, surely it is beyond time to try to sort out the main problems of over-crowding and lack of purpose which result in frustration, boredom, repressed anger and a bubbling hatred of the disgusting environment.

A government report entitled **"Safety in Custody Statistics, England and Wales: Deaths in Prison Custody to June 2024. Assaults and Self-harm to March 2024."** was published on **July 25th 2024** and we hear that whilst the number of deaths decreased over the last 12 months in custody, the number of individuals who self-harmed increased. This report also says that the rate of assaults increased from the previous 12-month period, the rate of assaults on staff increased from the previous 12-month period, the rate of serious assaults increased and 11% of all assaults were serious.

Pia Sinha CEO of the Prison Reform Trust said that *"Today's figures are a shameful reflection of just how far safety in our prisons has fallen. In the last year alone, we have seen more self-harming, by more people, more often; and further rises in assaults between prisoners, and on staff. The government has a serious task ahead to try to restore safety and stability to our jails.*

"When prisons are this overcrowded, and staff this overstretched, they become completely ill-equipped to deal with the scale of trauma and despair amongst the people in their care. The government has thankfully recognised the importance of reducing overcrowding as an immediate first step; this will buy some breathing space.

"But with the prison population projected to rise further still, attention will quickly need to turn to implementing longer term measures to reduce demand. Only then will we be able to break free of this downward spiral of declining safety in our prisons."

Rory Stewart, responding to the findings of openDemocracy, said they *"really help to make the case for a very important, moral reform that goes to the heart of our culture".* He added: *"[The investigation] confirms that prisons are perhaps the most shameful single aspect of society."* There are many charities working hard to improve literacy skills in prisons such as the Prison Education Trust, The Longford Trust, Nacro, The Howard League for Penal Reform and The Prison Reform Trust. I now see a new government initiative called **'The New Prison Education Service'** which was published on the 29th September 2023 and which will be an *"Overhaul of learning behind bars to include specialist teaching staff, apprenticeships and digital reading tools."* This they say will cut crime. But I refer them to the above reports. As I say over and over again, if prisons are so disgusting, so over-crowded, so under-resourced and so under-staffed this is just not going to happen. We have indeed heard it all before. Meanwhile our prisons are revolving doors for the vulnerable, the poor, the mentally ill, the illiterate, the forgotten, the isolated, the homeless, and the unloved.

Until all of these issues are addressed nothing will change.

ON REMAND

This is yet one more reason why our prisons are unnecessarily full.

According to figures published by the '**Offender Management Statistics Bulletin, England and Wales Quarterly: October to December 2023- 25 April 2024**' and published on the **25th April 2024**, nearly one-fifth (17%) of the prison population is on remand. This is a significant increase from 13% in 2023 and is the highest figure for 50 years.

Currently there are 16,458 people on remand and roughly one-third will be innocent of the original charge.

Innocent until proven guilty is an ancient principle of English law but we have already seen how you can be arrested for a crime you did not commit and be in no doubt that the few I have written about are just the tip of the iceberg.

Hopefully if you have been charged, whilst you are waiting for a court hearing or a trial you will be given bail. This means that you will be free to go back to your home until the hearing or trial begins. You might have to agree to certain conditions but basically you won't be locked up.

Once you have attended a hearing at a magistrates court however your actual trial could be delayed for months and the court might decide that you will be remanded in custody for however long it takes to get to court. And in 2023 some on remand were waiting for five years before they got to trial. That is five years of not being convicted of a crime. Even if found guilty the actual sentence could be shorter than this. As of 31 December 2023 data obtained under freedom of information laws by the charity 'Fair Trials' shows that at least 150 people – all male – had spent five years waiting to face a jury.

No wonder that the first question many defence barristers get asked when visiting the offender in the magistrates court is *"Will I get bail?"*

It would appear that too often, due to heavy workload or insufficient evidence and insufficient time, bail is unfairly refused. In **2016** a research report into pre-trial detention found many inaccuracies about previous convictions, a lack of witness statements, and sometimes not even the charge sheet setting out the exact nature of the crime was obtained by the defence counsel. A premium is put on speed rather than thoroughness and preparation. So while communications between the CPS and the police are notoriously slow due partly to the fact that in modern Britain, CPS areas that work in partnership with more than one force often have to manage more than one IT system, bail applications made in the Crown Courts are usually made at twenty-four hours' notice.

I see a charity called 'Transform Justice' and on their web site they say they are *"a national charity campaigning for a fairer, more humane, more open and effective justice system. Given this, there's a presumption that those pleading not guilty should be granted bail, so they can live in the community while waiting for their trial".*

They acknowledge that *"Speedy, summary justice has led to speedy remand. It may be necessary to slow down justice in order to improve decision-making."*

They also say that lawyers spoke to them about the disappearance of prison bail information services. Now the role of the Bail Information Officer is to provide relevant, objective, information to the court to assist decisions regarding bail. It is important to note that they do not advocate bail but gather and provide information to assist that decision making process.

They will need to interview the defendant, verify the details, compile a report, contact the defence barrister and liaise with other agencies.

But of the lawyers surveyed by 'Transform Justice', many said they had no experience whatsoever of bail information officers, 37% said they were never contacted by bail information officers and 46% said they were very rarely/not often contacted by them. The Bail Act is over 40 years old now and really needs to be totally reviewed.

So bail is refused and you are now remanded in a category B prison for an indeterminate length of time.

Security in Category B Prisons is robust but less stringent than in Category A prisons. Measures include high perimeter walls, CCTV surveillance, controlled entry points, and rigorous prisoner monitoring. They are supposed to offer education and other amenities but like everywhere else they are over-crowded and underfunded.

And in a recent report by the **House of Commons Justice Committee published in January 2023** I read that *"The justice system is ill-equipped to deal with ever-rising numbers of remand prisoners. Despite facing similar challenges to the wider prison population there is little support for remand prisoners either in prison or on release. The Committee calls for greater use of community alternatives to custodial remand, particularly for non-violent offences, and improved support for those subject to custodial remand."*

But we have seen the failings of the community sentencing structures so where do we go from here?

They go on to acknowledge what everyone already knows.

"The increase in the number of remand prisoners is placing severe pressure on an already struggling prison system and the report warns that entire prisons risk becoming dedicated to remand prisoners by default. Remand prisoners do not automatically receive the same level of support as the sentenced prison population. They are held in Category-B prisons which have some of the worst conditions and overcrowding in the prison estate. Upon leaving prison, remand prisoners face many of the same challenges reintegrating into their communities as those convicted of a crime, however they are not given the same level of support. Those found not guilty at trial are not entitled to any support at all on release."

You might want to read that last sentence again. You have lost maybe five or more years of your life. You have been locked up in a squalid unhealthy environment, you have probably been bullied, assaulted and isolated, and maybe lost your health, your job, your partner, your children and your home.

And you are not guilty.

So at last you walk out of prison a free man or woman or, yes, a child. You get no compensation and no support whatsoever to help you put together the shattered remnants of your life, not even an apology.

So this grand and important committee calls for *"greater support for remand prisoners. As a minimum, the prison service should ensure they receive the same access to mental health services, drug treatment, education and training as the rest of the prison population, and that their entitlements to visits are met. More investment is also needed in the prison estate to improve the conditions in Category B prisons to alleviate current overcrowding and understaffing. The Ministry of Justice also needs to ensure that there is adequate support available on release, particularly for accommodation services. Furthermore, those who are acquitted should be entitled to the same discharge grant as those who are sentenced and then released."*

I get so angry when I read those fine words. These people think they are so important but they then appear to walk away and don't involve themselves with these situations ever again. This report was published 18 months ago and so far as I can see, nothing has changed.

In fact today (**21st July 2024**) I read this:-

> "*Almost two-thirds of the 1,009 children on remand to youth detention centres did not later receive custodial sentences according to the 'Times Commission on Crime and Justice'. Nine in ten were in their exam years.*"

So more young lives destroyed by lack of concern and care.

'Action for Children' is another wonderful charity which helps all children in poverty and one of its specific aims is to "*support young people to access learning and jobs, we help criminally exploited children and young offenders turn their lives around, we campaign for them, and we step in to help stop young people becoming homeless.*"

Paul Cranberry of 'Action for Children' said "*All the research has told us prison does not work.*"

In 2022, Simon Hattenstone, a features writer for *the Guardian* wrote an article on remand prisoners in UK prisons. He reported that between 2012 and 2021, 265 prisoners awaiting trial or sentencing took their own lives.

What a shocking statistic. All these people could have been innocent, but still the number of those on remand increases.

Then I see an article in the online law magazine 'the Justice Gap' by Rona Epstein who is an honorary research fellow at Coventry School of Law. She writes in **December 2023** and reports on research done by the legal charity 'JUSTICE' who sent observers to 742 magistrates court hearings throughout England. They were looking at pre-trial remand hearings.

The chief problems, they found, was that four out of five decisions to remand in custody or impose bail conditions did not reference the relevant law and did not give full reasons with reference to the facts of the case, as is required under the Bail Act 1976. Well we have already seen that this can often be the case and it is such a major decision with such extreme consequences that it was felt that much more time should be given to this procedure. In one case, Rona Epstein says, the decision to impose a custodial sentence took just two minutes. Two minutes to deprive you of your liberty for maybe years, without trial.

Then again it was discovered that many defendants had a low understanding of the English language and of course were utterly confused with the whole legal process.

Often there were no interpreters present, but as **the Criminal Procedure Rules and section 5 of the Bail Act** states *"Ensuring that defendants understand processes involving them is best practice across courts and procedures, but in the remand decision-making context there is a specific requirement to explain decisions to defendants in language they can understand."* This certainly doesn't appear to be always happening.

As Rona Epstein says the whole remand system needs urgent reform.

And on 30th August 2024 I hear from the Centre of Crime and Justice Studies that there is to be a Private Members' Bill next week, the first week back after the summer recess, by the Labour peer Lord Woodley: the Imprisonment for Public Protection (Resentencing) Bill. They say that if it becomes law, this Bill *"will place the Justice Secretary under a legal obligation to ensure that all those serving an IPP sentence, whether in prison or in the community, are retrospectively given a determinate sentence. For the vast majority of IPP prisoners this will result in their swift and more than justified release."*

Oh my word that is such good news. This would be the equivalent of four medium sized men's prisons. It is absolutely a no-brainer.

It will take some time because there will be three readings in the Lords followed by three readings in the Commons.

But we are watching and listening Sir Keir. As they say, if all those who are currently in prison, due to unfair and heavy-handed decisions, were released tomorrow the over-crowding issue would be sorted.

RESETTLEMENT

So, at last, the day you have been waiting for has come and you are about to be released from the shackles of prison. Do you leap out with hope and excitement? Well I think we know enough to understand that that is probably not the case.

If you come out and you have nowhere to live, that means you don't have an address, so then you can't get a bank account and you won't have any credit records, so you can't rent because a landlord won't take you. If you haven't got your national insurance number you won't be able to claim benefits and even if you do have all that you need in order to put in a claim, it can often take weeks before you receive anything.

Prisoners are given a one off payment as they leave prison called a discharge grant, which for twenty-five years was £46 which was supposed to last until their benefits are paid. However in **2021** Robert Buckland decided to increase this to £76. You might get a travel warrant or voucher for transport to your home address if you have a home to go to. But the reality is more like this: *"I had to spend £18 on a cab to get to probation on time. Then I bought some food and it [the discharge grant] was gone. It took me seven weeks to get any more money because I was trying to sort a bank account, which you need for Universal Credit."*

Charities working with prison leavers have emphasised that financial hardship can be a factor that pushes people into reoffending straight after release. According to the Ministry of Justice, reoffending now constitutes 80% of all cautions and convictions and costs an estimated £18 billion per year.

The Howard League for Penal Reform has a really important scheme whereby they help young offenders with free legal advice. Their legal team operates a legal advice line for children and young people in prison. This is a free and confidential phone number.

They have also written a comprehensive guide on resettlement law for all practitioners who aim to support young people and help them with accommodation. Children have rights under the United Nations Convention on the Rights of the Child where it is stated that a child is defined as anyone under the age of 18, and it is apparent that in the UK prisons of today, some of these right are not being met.

I love this statement from Tabitha Kassem, former Legal Director of the Howard League where she says *"The law is not just a means of negative enforcement to put children and young people in prison; it can be a tool for positive change when they are released."*

And as Juliet Lyon, when Director of the Prison Reform Trust said, *"It doesn't make social or economic sense to imprison people only to release them a few months later ready to offend again. Solutions lie in responsible resettlement and agencies working together to help people lead a law abiding life back in their communities."*

44% of all prisoners are reconvicted within a year of their release. (I might have mentioned this before!) She calls for the Ministry of Justice to work across government departments and local authorities to put in place housing, employment, health and social care and family support groups which all contribute to successful rehabilitation on discharge. Hardly rocket science I would have thought.

Indeed back as far as **2012** there is a report by the Prison Reform Trust which gives the main reasons for reoffending. They are homelessness, drug addiction, illiteracy and lack of any employment.

MENTAL HEALTH

We also know that many people in prison suffer from mental illness and they obviously need so much support when discharged from prison. And yet another amazing charity is there to help. It is called **'Mind the Gap: supporting prison leavers with mental illness.'**

In some research which they did, led by Manchester University, they found that very few prisoners who had left prison with severe and enduring mental health conditions were still in contact with mental health services six months later. The study concluded that there *"is a need for robust discharge planning and proactive through care for prisoners with mental health problems"*.

This research was published in March **2024.** Over and over again wherever we look in the prison estate we hear the urgent call for reform.

'Mind the Gap' talk about an American model of care which is designed for patients leaving psychiatric hospital with nowhere to live. It is called 'Critical Time Intervention' (CTI) and the researchers from the University of Manchester wanted to know if this model could be applied to prisons. It involves the development of holistic discharge packages, to organise all the services and needs that patients have said are a priority to them. This includes funding, accommodation, education, and employment alongside healthcare needs. Well it sounds brilliant. The CTI managers (who are mainly nurses) work with patients both before and for a short period following their discharge, to ensure they have stable pathways and support in place.

Adapting it for prisons they ensured that prisoners on remand were able to attend court dates with arrangements in place (such as medication supplies, appointment with community services) should they be released. They registered prison leavers with GP services in the areas they were discharged to and they liaised with statutory and third sector organisations, plus families and other community links, around providing accommodation, where this was possible.

But they also say that *"CTI has not been widely adopted to date, in part due to higher costs than the standard model of release. However, given that it showed significantly better outcomes for prison leavers with severe mental health issues, it is likely that its use could lead to net savings overall, through wider economic benefits to public services through lower use of emergency care, better community integration, and reduced rates of reoffending".*

Oh my goodness how often do we hear that? Spend money now to save money in the future. They say that *"The Ministry of Justice should commission research to investigate the wider health economics of CTI."*

Yes, well the Ministry of Justice is going to be extremely busy over the next decade or two. In fact the previous governments also actually admits that not enough is done.

In the **"Seventy-eighth report of Session 2022-23 Ministry of Justice. Resettlement support for prison leavers,"** they say that *"HMPPS's resettlement services are not as effective or consistent as they should be, leading to inequalities for prison leavers."*

And the HMPPS says it *"is committed to ensuring that resettlement services provide consistent and adequate support to prison leavers, to reduce reoffending and protect the public."*

If only reports were read and words were acted upon we would have the best justice system in the world.

For then we get the report from the **National Audit Office in May 2023.**

I pick out just a few sentences.

They say that *"one of the core purposes of prison and probation services is to prepare prisoners for release effectively and ensure their smooth resettlement into the community. However, HMPPS and its partners across government do not do so consistently."*

Then they go on to say what we have already discovered which is that much of this problem is caused by staff shortages and an excessively high workload.

In December 2022, 1,762 out of 6,158 probation officer roles were unfilled.

This must date back to when Chris Grayling was Secretary of State for Justice and he decided to part-privatise the PPS.

Andrea Coomber KC (Hon.), Chief Executive of the Howard League for Penal Reform, said:-

> *"This report is a wake-up call. A bloated prison system means scarce resources are being used to build more jails – rather than improving rehabilitation services and ensuring people don't reoffend when returning to the community. There is a mismatch in public spending priorities and the end result is a system that sets people up to fail, rather than helping them move on from crime and lead positive lives. "Overstretched and under-resourced services are struggling under intolerable pressure. Severe staff shortages in prisons are leaving people locked in their cells with nothing to do, and severe staff shortages in Probation are making it harder for them to find a home and a job when they are released. "This will only get worse if the government proceeds with its plans to increase the prison population and build more prisons. Any serious attempt to reduce crime would begin with investment in housing, education and jobs instead."*

That, actually, says it all.

THE CRIMINAL

JUSTICE SYSTEM

*"**T**he current state of our criminal justice system should terrify us."* So says the Secret Barrister in the book of the same name which was written in **2018**. (And I will just record the fact that this book has reached number 92 in the top 100 bestselling books of the last fifty years.)

Nothing which has happened in the following years has improved the situation. The British criminal justice system used to be the gold-standard for the rest of the world but not anymore. There have been drastic cuts in legal aid, the backlog of cases is rising every day, barristers have been on strikes and the infrastructure of our courts is crumbling and is not fit for purpose.

Anyone involved with the criminal bar will respond with complete disgust and anger at the name of one person: (blood pressure alert) Chris Grayling.

He was responsible for the cuts in legal aid which came into effect on 1st April **2013**. This was part of a plan to save £350 million a year and meant that some types of case were no longer eligible for public funds - including divorce, child contact, welfare benefits, employment, clinical negligence, and housing law except in very limited circumstances.

But critics warned that the changes would be damaging. They said that these proposals were not survivable for the vast majority of the legal profession and that our country's position at the forefront of legal reputation would disappear overnight.

Not only would this mean that many junior barristers and smaller firms would go out of business but many vulnerable people would be forced to represent themselves in court.

A report in **2016** by Amnesty International begins with these words:-

> *"Every day, ordinary people face legal problems where they need to be able to get the right advice and support as soon as possible. Be it a parent trying to secure contact with their child, a disabled person who has had her benefits wrongly cut, or an 18-year-old born in the UK who is trying to regularise his immigration status or claim her entitlement to British citizenship. Without that advice and support the consequences can be profound: they could face being made homeless, falling deeply into debt, being prevented from seeing their children, or being separated from their families. This has a significant human cost for the individuals themselves and their families, and a wider cost to society as other services have to take the strain of supporting people whose problems have spiralled out of control. These are some of the consequences of the severe cuts to civil legal aid that were included in the 2012 Legal Aid, Sentencing and Punishment of Offenders (LASPO) Act. The upshot of those changes is a two-tier justice system: open to those who can afford it, but, increasingly closed to the poorest, most vulnerable and most in need of its protection."*

Indeed in the book *"Fake Law"* by the Secret Barrister we hear that the government readily admitted that the removal of legal aid from most welfare law would have a 'disproportionate impact on disabled people' but considered it a price worth paying. (Dr. J. Organ and Dr. J. Sigafoos, **'The impact of LASPO on routes to**

justice, Equalities and Human Rights Commission Sept 2018). Worth paying for whom I ask?

And on 5th September 2024, we are still hearing about the ongoing disastrous effects of these cuts in legal aid. This time particularly on children.

We hear a strong warning from 'Resolution' which is a community of family justice professionals who work with families and individuals to resolve issues in a constructive way. 'Resolution' was founded in 1982 by a group of family lawyers who believed that a non-confrontational approach to family law issues would produce better outcomes for separating families and their children.

Their chairman , Grant Cameron, has said that *"family courts are at breaking point with demand "higher than ever"* and he says that families are having to endure *"massive delays."* Nick Emmerson, president of the Law Society, also highlights the *"dire state"* of the family court noting that thousands of children are forced to wait almost a year in limbo as they are failed by a system that should protect them.

And the main reason for this appalling delay is put squarely at the cuts in legal aid in 2012. As Jenny Beck, a family law solicitor and co-chair of the Legal Aid Practitioners Group says, *"The removal of legal aid from 80% of family cases has been a complete false economy."*

So Chris Grayling is personally responsible for the trauma being suffered by children as the family courts struggle to cope.

But these cuts also meant that barristers and solicitors were hit with 30 per cent cuts in fees for the most complex fraud cases – known as Very High Cost Cases (VHCCs). And in December 2013 barristers from 17 different chambers refused to take on a fraud case because of the reduced pay rates.

Oh my word the media didn't approve of that.

So this warranted a letter from me to *The Times* which was published on the **27th December 2013.**

They called it *"Legal Jeopardy"*

Sir, You say ("Barristers say 'no' and put fraud trials in jeopardy," Dec23rd) that 17 chambers have refused to provide barristers for a very complicated fraud case. What a disgraceful state of affairs. And how has this been allowed to happen? Cut after cut in legal aid, and a government and justice secretary who refuse to listen to genuine concerns from the legal profession. There has been a vote of no confidence in the chief executive and president of the Law Society by the solicitors, and criminal barristers will be 'on strike' on January 6th,. This from a profession who never normally get together to protest. What more do they have to do to underline the seriousness of their concerns that the best legal system in the world is now under threat?

I obviously didn't let the celebrations of Christmas dampen down my anger.

And then we hear of another very high profile case on the **1st May 2014** which was also having to be abandoned due to cuts in legal aid.

This was a £5million fraud case which was also extremely complex.

The barrister who was representing seven defendants in this trial, known as 'Operation Cotton,' and was doing it free of charge, applied to have the trial stopped because cuts to legal aid meant that his clients could not find barristers of *"sufficient competence."* The interesting thing was that the barrister who called a halt to the proceedings was Alex Cameron QC, none other than the brother of the then prime minster.

Mr. Cameron laid the blame for the lack of legal representation at the door of his brother's government – saying the problem was widespread in court cases, and that the state had *"failed"*.

He said: *"We do attribute the fault to the state more widely. The problem is this case is not the only case that has this problem. At the moment there is a finite resource [of barristers] and too much capacity required. "Is the position going to be that this case should swallow up the available silks... .....so that these other cases are adjourned or stayed?"*

This case put cuts to legal aid, implemented by Justice Secretary Chris Grayling, very much in the spotlight.

And it also produced yet another letter to *The Times* from me!

This one was published on **8th August 2014** and was called:

"Crisis at the Bar"

Sir, We really do need to tell young people not to do a law degree at all if they think it is going to lead to employment at the Bar. It will indeed be a waste of money. Defence barristers are leaving the Bar in droves, because it is such a shambles. Cuts in legal aid, late payment for work done years ago, inefficiency by the CPS, all contribute to a profession in crisis. It is becoming impossible to make a living at the Bar unless you are one of the very few at the top.

So the legal system is still trying to recover from these draconian cuts and Chris Grayling is now, thank goodness, no longer an MP.

Oh but wait a moment. Just one hour before voting closed at the general election on the 4th July, Sunak handed him a peerage in his dissolution honours list. So he is now a member of the House of Lords and will be known as the Rt Hon. Lord Grayling. I have no words.

The justice department has now (**2024**) got a new Justice Secretary who we hope will be in the post for very many years. Under the past Conservative government this department was never given the importance it deserved.

In October **2021** Dominic Raab became the tenth justice secretary since Lord Falconer in **2007.** The longest any politician who has been in the job since then was the Labour MP Jack Straw at 2 years and 10 months. Liz Truss was there for just over 10 months and David Liddington was there for just over 6 months. Michel Gove, Rory Stewart and David Gauke all had tenures of under 18 months. So basically no one had the time to think about reforming the criminal justice system or our prisons.

Such a shame that none of them seemed to have heard the wise words of the Lord Chief Justice Lord Burnett of Maldon when he said in **November 2021** that *"the courts are not a service like any other. They do not exist simply to provide a service to those who use them. They are one of the foundations of the rule of law and one of the building blocks on which civil society and economic activity rests."*

But Dominic Raab **did** have the time to spend some of our money. In 2021 he wasted £238 million which was an increase of 14 times on the year before. £98.2 million was on an electronic tagging system which the Prison and Probation Service eventually scrapped and a further £14 million was paid to companies that used local probation services after their contracts were broken early even though they failed to reduce re-offending.

Maybe if he hadn't wasted so much money on useless projects he would have been able to prevent a strike by criminal barristers.

On the 11th April **2022** they went on strike for the first time in their history. Jo Sidhu KC (then QC) chair of the Criminal Bar Association said that a junior barrister starting out on his career earns about £12,000 a year after he has paid his expenses. He said that the pay increase offered by the Secretary of State was completely inadequate. They were striking initially on alternate weeks in a dispute over pay, working conditions and legal aid funding. But then having rejected the offer of a 15% rise, on the 22 August 2022 they voted to go on an indefinite and uninterrupted strike from September 5th.

Solicitors too were impacted by this and the President of the Law Society at the time, Lubna Shuja, said that *"We are extremely concerned that for many of our members there could be no viable future in criminal defence practice. It is a tragedy for the British justice system that years of political neglect have forced us unavoidably to this conclusion. Dominic Raab has made the wrong decision in not implementing the immediate 15% criminal legal aid rate rise for solicitors. The independent review recommended this a year ago as a bare minimum to prevent the criminal defence sector from collapsing,"* She went on to say that, *"Until the government chooses to address the collapse of the criminal justice system, victims will continue to be let down and talk of being tough on crime will be nothing but hot air."*

So of course trials were delayed and the courts were in complete disarray and it wasn't until Raab had gone and Brandon Lewes became Justice Secretary that a new offer was accepted by the barristers. Now Brandon Lewes was in the job for just over one month! This was due to the rapid turnover of leadership at the top. So things can move on very quickly if the will is there. But uncertainty, lack of responsibility and lack of accountability continues to pervade the criminal justice system.

And now there is a huge backlog of trials and delays have never been so long. The backlog seemed to start in 2019 when the government decided to cap the number of cases when judges could sit to hear cases. This was partly because of predictions about falling crime rates but also surprise, surprise, to save money.

Well there was a very slight reduction of all prosecutions in 2019 of only about 1% and it actually seemed very short- sighted at the time.

But then I see that there was much more to it than just that.

I said at the beginning of this book that this is my personal journey through the prisons and justice system of this country but it is becoming more like a voyage of discovery. In the years between **2010 and 2019** I, like most people, would just hear snippets of news about courts and barristers and I would then get on with my life. But now, delving a bit further, the detail is actually shocking.

One huge issue which is in need of reform is the Single Justice Procedure. These are court hearings which are held in secret with no journalists or media present. They were introduced in 2015 in order to speed up the system and to fast-track the prosecution of low-level offences. But it has resulted in a huge number of people being criminalised unfairly. Cases are often decided by a single magistrate at top speed, often without the defendant present. Offences such as non-payment of television licence fees, speeding, and even those with dementia who have not paid certain bills and victims of domestic abuse have been affected by these secret courts. Very often the mitigating letters explaining health problems and personal difficulties from the defendants were not read.

And in August 2024 a top judge ruled that 75,000 convictions for rail fare evasion would have to be overturned after a huge misuse of this system across seven years was uncovered. Speed is the enemy of a fair and transparent criminal justice system and sentencing must be scrutinized by all those involved. Lord Thomas of Cwmgiedd, a former lord chief justice has said that the secretive Single Justice Procedures were "*tilted against fairness*" and should be overhauled.

Overhauled? The whole system should be scrapped NOW.

In **2016** the government continued to try to modernise and streamline the justice system and according to the Law Society in an article in January 2024, over half the courts across England and Wales were closed down.

Many of these courts were small, old, crumbling and unsatisfactory buildings and some were under-used, and the idea was to sell them off and make loads of money in order to fund a new, modern, digitalized, technical, and probably *"world beating"* court system. Wow this sounds marvellous. However I have always found it to be a good idea to explore in more detail further various plans which sound just a bit too good to be true. And indeed it is just a bit worrying when you hear that this programme is seen as being hugely ambitious, is going to cost £1.2 billion, and in fact has never been attempted anywhere else before. The Public Accounts Committee has said that these changes will be extremely challenging to deliver. The HM Courts & Tribunal Service (HMCTS) who are enacting these changes have already extended its timetable from four to six years and has only delivered two-thirds of what is expected by now.

As they say, the pressure is on to deliver quickly in order to try to make savings but this leads to dangerous short- cuts. The revised six-year timescale for the reforms is still shorter than the time taken to complete smaller programmes in other countries.

Then a report from the National Audit Office in **2019** found that *"there had been less progress than expected, expected costs had increased and planned benefits had decreased. Delays in introducing primary legislation created a significant degree of uncertainty."*

The report recommended that HMCTS should:

- *"allow enough time to engage with affected parties within the justice system;*
- *resist pressure to claim savings until planned changes are fully embedded;*
- *provide greater transparency of its objectives and progress; and*
- *work with the Ministry of Justice and HM Treasury to address the system-wide consequences of planned changes."*

Well that all sounds eminently sensible to me. But we need to think about the human costs to this work.

On the **16th May, 2019**, members of Justice Alliance, a campaign group, and other practitioners, congregated opposite the site of the former Bloomsbury County Court, holding candles as they watched a slideshow highlighting the fate of some of the 162 magistrates' and 62 county courts that have closed and they called for a moratorium on the closure of any more courts. As they point out, the closure of so many courts means that people have to travel much further in order to reach court. This puts huge pressure on people with child care concerns, those without private transport and those in rural communities, those with little financial support or those who own a business. Travel time is not paid for so that could mean extra costs such as overtime pay for staff. Those who may need an interpreter might also be less willing to attend court. And of course local courts are much easier for those with disability or mobility problems. And some of these groups may not be best served by a remote hearing.

Then I hear some further very sound advice. *"We believe that any technology used to replace physical hearings must be tested and shown to work before courts are closed."*

This is another sentence you might have to read again!

Please, why on earth does this need saying?

So we then look at the **NAO report in February 2023** by Gareth Davies head of the NAO to see exactly what progress has been made.

In their press release they say that: *"HMCTS has a limited understanding of whether reforms are delivering intended efficiencies. While it recorded a net total of £311m in savings from running costs between 2014-15 and 2021-22, it acknowledges that these figures may not be fully attributable to reform. Costs of running many services are higher than pre-reform and it lacks routine data on how efficiently reformed services are operating. Some services are not yet operating as expected. For example, many online divorce and probate cases needed manual interventions by court staff despite the relevant project being marked as complete. As yet, HMCTS has no overarching benefits realisation plan."*

Basically I think this means that no, there has not been sufficient progress and it all seems to have been a huge waste of money, resources and time.

Indeed all of that money could have been better spent repairing and maintaining the courts' infrastructure. It is in a disgraceful state.

The Law Society conducted a review of lawyers still managing to work in the system just two years ago in 2022. They speak about the physical conditions of the courts and here are some descriptions in their own words.

- *"Everything is falling apart. Chairs and floors are held together with gaffer tape. Ceilings leak, toilets leak and fail to flush. Mould everywhere."* (Inner Crown Court, London)
- *"The standards of cleanliness, access to drinking water, heating/air conditioning and physical infrastructure are appalling. Bio security is haphazard or non-existent. Access to internet is not reliable. Standards of comfort are non-existent. Rather than being regarded as officers of the court solicitors are treated as an inconvenience."* (Brighton)
- *"Depends which venue. I've had a piece of an air conditioning unit fall on my head at a magistrates court a few years ago and the ceiling fan it fell from still hadn't been mended when I last went."* (Manchester)
- *"It's derelict. Not fit for purpose. The courts have been neglected since I have been attending since 1991. They are embarrassing. At Birkenhead half the building has fallen down and the other half is closed due to asbestos. I could talk for hours about the appalling state of our courts."* (Liverpool)

Many had experienced delays to cases due to the state of buildings in 2022.

It would seem that in spite of so-called good intentions by the Conservative government we haven't advanced since the days of Charles Dickens.

Then we see a report by the Bar Council which highlighted conditions in a Welsh Court which was infested with fleas, a court which had sewage flowing down the walls and a London court where a barrister had to conduct a hearing holding an umbrella over his head because of a leaking roof.

And do you remember the Nightingale hospitals which were built at top speed during the pandemic but were actually hardly ever used?

Well the following is making a lot of people very cross.

Nightingale Courts were hurriedly set up to address the pandemic backlog at a cost of £34m, and (ready for this?) some were actually located in the former court buildings that had been closed by Tory governments since 2010 in order to save money.

There must be a TV psycho drama here somewhere. You couldn't make it up and you wouldn't have to.

So of course the result of all this incompetence means that the backlog continued to grow and by December 2020, the Crown Court backlog hit a record of more than 57,000 cases. By December 2021, it had grown to 58,204. And that year, the average time taken to deal with cases hit a record of just over two years at 780 days.

But today (25th July 2024) there are reports of a case which involves several defendants and alleged offences dating from 2019 having a trial set for October 2027 as the crown court backlog continues to grow. This is unprecedented. Of course you will hear the Tory government blaming the pandemic and the barrister's strikes for this but the real reason is lack of funding, total ignorance and gross stupidity. These dreadful delays are causing victims of crime to withdraw their support for the prosecutions resulting in cases collapsing. This situation is particularly acute in relation to rape and serious sexual offences. (RASSO)

Retention and recruitment of expert RASSO counsel is a prime contributor to the many problems in the system. These particular lawyers are not paid for 50% of the work involved. Indeed many barristers have to fight to get the pay they are owed on a variety of cases. The backlog of rape cases is expected to reach 3,000 by the end of March 2025 which would be a five-fold increase on the pre-pandemic figure.

But the entire backlog of all cases in the crown courts has now reached more than 68,000 and will probably rise to 70,000 by March 2025, whilst in the magistrates' courts the figure is an alarming 387,042.

In June 2024 the president of the Law society in England and Wales, Nick Emmerson, said *"It is alarming to see the criminal court backlogs continue to spiral. It is unacceptable that victims, witnesses and defendants are having to wait so long, with their lives in limbo, to access justice. The criminal justice system is in crisis with huge backlogs of cases, crumbling courts and overcrowded prisons. "There simply are not enough judges and lawyers to work on all the cases and we have heard concerning reports that court buildings are not being used to their full capacity".*

We hear this all the time. Experienced judges and barristers are leaving the profession in droves and there are not enough new lawyers entering the profession. A report by the National Audit Office in May this year highlighted the decline in lawyers working in the criminal defence profession which they say *"is due to a reduction in legal aid fees, increasing levels of stress and poor working conditions."* It also pointed to the *"dilapidated state of much of the court estate and the failure to deliver prisoners to court on time as factors which only add to the delays. Sustained investment across the criminal justice system must be a priority for the next UK government."*

We go back to **2022** when the Law Society was saying this:-

Our legal system is world leading, our court estate should be too. We're calling on the government to:-

- *invest in buildings and staff*
- *properly fund legal aid*
- *keep cases out of the courtroom*
- *ensure technology is reliable*
- *collect better data*

And now in September 2024 we hear about a report just published by the Bar Council. It is calling for the budget of the Ministry of Defence to be boosted in any forthcoming spending review. They say that funding for justice was more than 30% below where it would be if it had kept pace with UK inflation. The chairman, Sam Townend KC, said that its findings would not *"come as a surprise to all those who work within the justice system."*

Well it won't come as surprise to anyone who has read this book.

He goes on to say that *"Crumbling court buildings, barristers and solicitors leaving publicly funded practice as fees have stagnated, swingeing cuts to legal aid leaving litigants in person struggling to represent themselves. And all of this exacerbates the chronic problem of court backlogs."*

So two years later things have only got worse.

No-one listens. No-one cares.

ALL CHANGE

But what is this I am hearing? Amazing things are happening and one of them is the most exciting event involving prison reform for decades.

I am writing this on the 7th July 2024 and three days ago we had a General Election. Sir Keir Starmer's Labour Party won a huge majority and they have hit the ground running. That was on Thursday so today is Sunday. Just to give you a flavour of the man, he has already abolished the Rwanda scheme, he has appointed real experts in various departments, he has given an excellent press conference, he has held a cabinet meeting, and he is visiting Scotland, N. Ireland, and Wales before flying to Washington on Tuesday for a NATO summit. His entire team are already at their desks except for the new foreign secretary who is already in Berlin discussing closer ties with the EU. People are saying that there has been more progress in the last three days than in the last 14 years.

But as if this was all not exciting enough it is the appointment of James Timpson as prisons' minister which is sending everyone who cares about prison reform into the absolute paroxysms of delight. I have already mentioned him, so who is this man?

James Timpson is a member of the Timpson family shoe business. He has been Chief Executive of the Timpson Group, owned by his father John Timpson, since 2002. It is the largest service retailer in the UK, with 1300 shops across the UK and Ireland. Its main services include key cutting, shoe repairs, watch repairs, engraving, phone repairs, photo processing and dry cleaning. This family has an incredible work ethic whereby it leaves all their employees to do whatever they like. I watched James Timpson being interviewed and he said 'his employees only have to *"put money in the till and look the part"*; for the rest, they have complete authority to do whatever they think is right to offer a quality service to customers.' He said they can paint the store pink if they think that is the right thing to do. It makes for happy staff and happy staff bring in the money.

But he is also known for his policy of recruiting and rehabilitating ex- prisoners to work for him and he believes in giving people second chances. He became chairman of the Prison Reform Trust in 2016 and he firmly believes that only a third of all prisoners should be behind bars. In a blog he states that:-

> *"We can't keep locking up 85,000 people today knowing that hardly any of them will manage to find work and that around 50% of them will be back in again within a year of release. There are currently too many people in prison, and we have a system that seems to keep bringing them back there time and time again--that has to stop. Prison reform means fewer prisons and better prisoners."*

And again in the interview with Krishnan Guru-Murthy of Channel 4, he said *"the UK is addicted to sentencing and punishment."* He went on to say that: *"A lot of people in prison in my view shouldn't be there, and they are there for far too long. It's getting worse. There are people serving sentences for longer than they have been alive."* He then refers to systems in other countries where he thinks we could learn a lot. He says that *"Holland has shut half of their prisons. They have a different way of sentencing, it's community sentencing. They continue in society, and it makes them less likely to re-offend. Custodial sentences aren't always the right way."*

Indeed, when we start to look at other countries we find some very different approaches and I think it is really important to take note.

The test is the re-offending rate and we see this to be much lower than the UK in Sweden, Norway, Denmark, Finland and the

Netherlands for example. All of these countries have some of the lowest crime rates and lowest rates of recidivism in the world.

So let us look at some of these countries in turn and at their prison systems.

What do they have in common? Well they all have many open prisons and they try to keep people out of prison whenever possible. It is also generally accepted that punishment and rehabilitation go hand in hand, and that prisoners, no matter what their crime, have certain rights.

Baz Dreisinger is a professor and executive director of the 'Incarceration Nations Network' (INN) which is a *global network that supports, instigates and popularizes innovative prison reform and justice reimagining efforts around the world.*

She has an in-depth knowledge of criminal justice systems across the globe and she says that the important thing about the Nordic countries is that they *have excellent social services, which have important flow-on effects.*

Why, oh why, is this not recognized sufficiently in the UK?

"Because of strong social services, crime is less likely to occur," she says.

Also in these Nordic countries, the prisons can be found in the middle of towns and cities. *"So if you go to prison, it's highly likely ... your family will be able to see you with relative ease."*

But when crime does occur, these countries work hard to keep people out of the prison system.

"People don't automatically get sent to prisons as a knee-jerk, immediate response ... there's very strong mediation programs that are capable of diverting people out of the system to begin with," she says.

She talks about **Norway**.

Many of the characteristics of Nordic prisons that set them so far apart from other countries are because of a certain set of principles. The first is what's known as the principle of *"normality"*.

Dreisinger says the idea is that *"life inside prisons ought to resemble life outside as closely as possible"*.

> *"So that means wearing your own clothes, cooking in communal kitchens, having a fair amount of mobility in different spaces, having a cell that isn't really a cell but more of a dorm, and then very, very critically, receiving the same services that you would receive as if you were on the outside."*

Next up, the principle of *"reintegration"* or *"progression"*.

> *"There's a tremendous emphasis from day one on what's going to happen when you leave the system — when you come out, when you go home,"* She says.

Basically they seem to treat prisoners as humanely as possible. As I keep saying it is the deprivation of your liberty which is the 'punishment'.

All prisons in Norway offer education, drug treatment, mental health and training programmes. After release in Norway there is an emphasis on helping offenders reintegrate into society, with access to active labour market programmes set up to help ex-prisoners find a job and access to a variety of social support services such as housing, social assistance and disability insurance.

Of course they realise that some people have to be fully contained such as with the Breivnik case who, if you remember, killed 77 people in Norway in 2011. As Dreisinger says: *"If there are scenarios where someone is clearly a great danger to society, and needs to be deprived of liberty for extensive periods of time, that person will be held. It's just that that's not the starting point for the Norwegian system."*

But it is the amazing way they treat children which uplifts my soul. Their attitude couldn't be more different to that of the UK. Basically they very rarely send children to prison at all. As Dreisinger says: *"Sending a young person to detention is the absolute, complete last resort ... It [only] happens in extreme circumstances".*

In Norway, the age of criminal responsibility is 15 years old but even then, there's only a handful of under-18s behind bars who have committed serious crimes.

In the UK the age of criminal responsibility is 10 except in Scotland where it is 12.

Then we see what is happening in the **Netherlands.**

They say they are actually short of people to lock up. Whilst the UK plans to build more and more prisons, in the Netherlands, over the past few years, 19 prisons have closed down and more are due for closure in the coming years.

Angeline van Dijk, who is director of the prison service in the Netherlands, says jail is increasingly used for those who are too dangerous to release, or for vulnerable offenders who need the help available inside.

"Sometimes it is better for people to stay in their jobs, stay with their families and do the punishment in another way," she says. *"We have shorter prison sentences and a decreasing crime rate here in the Netherlands so that is leading to empty cells."*

But even in the high security prisons in the Netherlands the regime is very relaxed.

"In the Dutch service we look at the individual," says Jan Roelof van der Spoel, deputy governor of Norgerhaven, a high-security prison in the north-east of the Netherlands.

> *"If somebody has a drug problem we treat their addiction, if they are aggressive we provide anger management, if they have got money problems we give them debt counselling. So we try to remove whatever it was that caused the crime. The inmate himself or herself must be willing to change but our method has been very effective. Over the last 10 years, our work has improved more and more."*

This approach is so obviously sensible but I see no sign of it being looked at by the UK.

He adds that some persistent offenders - known in the trade as *"revolving-door criminals"* - are eventually given two-year sentences and tailor-made rehabilitation programmes. Fewer than 10% then return to prison after their release.

A decade ago the Netherlands had one of the highest incarceration rates in Europe, but it now claims one of the lowest - 57 people per 100,000 of the population, compared with 148 in England and Wales.

Then we see that in **Iceland** there are only five prisons, altogether housing fewer than 200 prisoners. Of course we need to understand that the population of Iceland is only 377,689. But the high standard of living, small population, common social bind against criminality, and a well-trained and highly educated police force are contributing factors to the low crime rate. They also have equal rights to the same education and the same schools so there is not a massive class system.

And once again we see the same holistic approach and the treatment of prisoners as individuals. They are encouraged to undertake significant roles within the prison community like mentoring or cooking and to keep up with maintaining family connections. Prisoners have their own room keys but they leave their doors unlocked, pretty much at all times in the knowledge that it won't be abused in any way.

As Professor Francis Pakes, from the University of Portsmouth's School of Criminology and Criminal Justice says. *"The UK has much to gain by adopting elements of Iceland's approach, moving towards a more humane and effective prison system."*

Absolutely but are they listening?

Then we get a similar situation in **Finland.** Prisoners get their own rooms, access to plenty of recreation and are transferred to open prisons quickly to prepare for their release. It's part of a long-standing policy aimed not at mollycoddling those inside, but at ensuring they don't come back.

As prison governor of Ojoinen prison Kaisa Tammi-Moilanen explains, the prison authorities have *"purposely tried to avoid everything that we can which are associated with a prison"*, which also means that there are no physical barriers stopping the prisoners from attempting to escape. Tammi-Moilanen explains that this is intentional, and is meant to encourage the prisoners to develop their own sense of self-control. This dual focus on rehabilitation and the development of self-sufficiency is the cornerstone of the Ojoinen experience, she says.

"When you put people into institutions like prisons, they become institutionalised. But we don't want this," Tammi-Moilanen explains. *"The key is that we try to give people the idea that it is possible to change, that there is hope."*

"Prisoners in a closed prison don't need to learn any self-control, because everything they do is controlled. But to be a normal citizen you need to have inner control of your life, so you know how to behave, you know what is good for you and you know what is good for the society."

It is just such an intelligent approach, it quite takes my breath away.

One of the inmates at Ojoinen prison says that *"Especially for the younger men, who have been involved in drugs, this system helps them to get their life on track. They become used to waking up early, going to work, and taking care of themselves, instead of taking drugs at night and lying in bed all day."*

A prisoner's typical weekday usually begins at 6am, when they wake up and have breakfast, before reporting to the prison reception for the morning roll-call.

By 7am, the prisoners are ready to begin their working day. A number of prisoners have jobs with local businesses, while the rest perform tasks organised by the prison.

This dual focus on rehabilitation and the development of self-sufficiency is the cornerstone of the Ojoinen experience, according to the prison's director Tammi-Moilanen, who has 28 years' experience of working in open and closed prisons across Finland.

Currently in Finland there are 11 open prisons and 15 closed prisons.

Of course it is inevitable that some think the Finnish law and punishments handed out by the Finnish courts is too lenient.

But the evidence does not back that up. It is a progressive system where a prisoner starts his or her sentence in a closed prison, moves later into an open prison, continues to electronic monitoring out in society and lastly to parole. It is a step-by-step process based on an individual sentence plan.

And when an inmate responded to a comment that it was like a holiday camp he said that after his release he has *"absolutely no intention of ever coming back"*.

Whatever your thoughts on these systems, one thing is clear: The rate of recidivism is much lower than in other countries.

Well I think we can see where we are going with all of this. Of course, as it is freely acknowledged, there will always be some people who have to be in secure custody accommodation for a very long time. But the way these prisons work are a million miles from the situation in the UK.

But this is music to our ears. At his press conference on Friday Starmer said that *"if young people, particularly boys, are offered support at a point of intervention in the early years it could ensure some of them do not get on that escalator to imprisonment."* He talked about knife crime and said he was determined to tackle this and said that he was so pleased that James Timpson was now the minister for prisons.

Well I think we can all agree to that and for the first time that I can remember we have someone who understands the situation and hopefully will be here for long enough to make a difference.

SO MANY WORDS

But sadly I am not able to close on that hopeful statement because I see more and more words from so many years ago to the present day.

I have quoted copiously from the reports by various chief Inspectors of prisons but I will now pick out just a few phrases from some annual reports since 2007.

"HM Chief Inspector of Prisons for England and Wales annual report 2007 to 2008."

Dame Anne Owers

"Safety in our expanding prisons is a growing concern. Rates of self-harm, particularly among younger women in prison, remain appallingly high. There have been more disturbances than last year, so far able to be contained. This year, too many of the most volatile of our prisons – especially dispersal prisons, holding an increasingly challenging mix of very serious offenders, and also those prisons that hold young men – were not judged on inspection to be sufficiently safe.

Many local prisons have accommodation that is entirely unsuitable, cramped or unhygienic. Mental disorder, learning disabilities and an ageing population are making huge demands on overstretched services and often unsuitable buildings: prisons will struggle to comply with their duties under the Disability Discrimination Act."

"The first of those lessons is the need to avoid un-thought-through and un-resourced legislation of the kind that produced the indeterminate sentence for public protection."

"The second lesson is the need to invest in alternatives to prison for those who do not need to be, and should not be, there. We await the results of the Bradley inquiry into mental health diversion, following our own mental health thematic review, as well as some concrete outcomes from the Corston report into women in the criminal justice system. More work is also needed to provide viable and sustainable alternatives for those serving short sentences. Recent research suggests prison can make a difference to predicted reoffending – but not for short-term prisoners, whose risks may indeed be increased by a disruptive custodial sentence."

"HM Chief Inspector of Prisons for England and Wales Annual Report 2011–12"

Nick Hardwick

"Progress on safety and respect appeared to have stalled. The number of self-inflicted deaths in prison rose from 54 (0.64 per 1,000 prisoners) in 2010–11 to 66 (0.76 per 1,000 prisoners) in 2011–12."

"When we compared survey results for prisons inspected this year with those from their previous inspections, prisoners' perceptions of their safety had significantly worsened in twice as many prisons as those where they had significantly improved."

"HM Chief Inspector of Prisons for England and Wales Annual Report 2013–14"

Nick Hardwick

"The overall level of assaults in prison increased in 2013–14 and the increase was particularly high in adult male prisons. The number of assaults involving adult male prisoners increased by 14% on the year before and was the highest for any year for which we have data. Adult male prisons are becoming more violent every year; that trend accelerated in 2013–14 and included a dramatic 38% rise in the number of serious assaults."

"HM Chief Inspector of Prisons for England and Wales Annual Report 2015–16"

Nick Hardwick

"What I have seen is that despite the sterling efforts of many who work in the Prison Service at all levels, there is a simple and unpalatable truth about far too many of our prisons. They have become unacceptably violent and dangerous places."

"Prisoners, including young adults, spent too much time locked in their cells."

"The annual report of HM Chief Inspector of Prisons from 1 April 2017 to 31 March 2018."

Peter Clarke

"The year 2017–18 was a dramatic period in which HM Inspectorate of Prisons documented some of the most disturbing prison conditions we have ever seen – conditions which have no place in an advanced nation in the 21st century. In this, my third annual report as HM Chief Inspector of Prisons for England and Wales, violence, drugs, suicide and self-harm, squalor and poor access to education are again prominent themes. Another recurrent theme is the disappointing failure of many prisons to act on our previous recommendations – which are intended

to help save lives, keep prisoners safe, ensure they are treated respectfully and to give a chance of returning to the community less likely to reoffend."

However, *"Across the service there are examples of good practice which we will play a part in sharing widely,"*

"The annual report of HM Chief Inspector of Prisons from 1 April 2019 to 31 March 2020."

Peter Clarke

"It is good to see that this year, for the first time since 2015–16, a slightly higher proportion of our recommendations have been achieved than not. I hope this sets a pattern for the future as it is clear the correlation applies to all types of prison. For instance, Cardiff is a local prison that has faced many challenges, so it was particularly pleasing to see strong improvement there in 2019."

However, (there always seems to be a 'however') *"Given the obvious linkage between excessive time locked in cells and mental health issues, self-harm and drug abuse, it was concerning to find that the amount of time for which prisoners were unlocked for time out of cell was often unacceptably poor. Nineteen per cent of adult male prisoners told us that they were out of their cells for less than two hours on weekdays, including 32% in men's local prisons. Is it any surprise that self-harm in prisons has been running at historically high levels during the past year? Prisoners often tell us they are harming themselves to gain some attention, for instance if their applications or complaints are being ignored."*

"In February 2017 I wrote to Dr. Philip Lee, the minister responsible for youth justice, pointing out that, at that time, there was no establishment we inspected that we could say was safe to hold children. This was shortly after the publication of

a report by Charlie Taylor, setting out a vision for children's custody centred around a concept of secure schools, where well-trained staff experienced in education, health and welfare would work with children in a supporting environment and where disincentives to learning should be avoided. Taylor's vision was broadly welcomed and secure schools were agreed by government as the blueprint for the future of children's custody. Nearly four years on, there is still no sign of secure schools becoming reality.

"Meanwhile, the outcomes for many children have been appalling. In January 2020 we published a thematic inspection report about the separation of children in custody, where children are unable to mix with their peers either to maintain order, as part of a punishment, due to the prison running a limited regime, or their own decision to self-isolate. The findings were, frankly, a disgrace."

Is anyone reading these dreadful reports?

"The annual report of HM Chief Inspector of Prisons from 1 April 2021 to 31 March 2022."

Charlie Taylor

'We have been struck by the long hours which many inmates have to spend locked in their cells in boredom. In several local prisons a proportion of the population, including un-convicted prisoners, were locked up for twenty-two hours or more each day, for weeks on end. In some training prisons, where a full working day was intended to be central to the life of the establishment, we found some of the population without any work and others employed on work which was unsatisfactory in nature or which was insufficient to support the number of prisoners allocated to it. We believe there are powerful reasons why Prison Department must ensure that an inmate does not spend day after day in blank inactivity; he should be kept occupied for a normal working day at work, education, or some

other constructive activity.'

"It is 40 years since this passage was published in the first annual report from HM Chief Inspector of Prisons and it remains as relevant now as it did in 1982. Each of my six predecessors has found a new form of words to describe this seemingly intractable problem.

"Some of the most disheartening inspections were at prisons with large proportions of young men, where the often extensive grounds and workshops remained mostly empty and just a handful of prisoners were receiving any face-to-face teaching. The failure to fill the gaps in the skills and education of these prisoners and the low expectations of their abilities and potential meant they were learning to survive in prison rather being taught how to succeed when they were released. Unless these men are given the support that they need, there is the potential that they will lead long lives of criminality – creating victims, disrupting their communities and placing a huge burden on the state."

"The annual report of HM Chief Inspector of Prisons from 1 April 2022 to 31 March 2023."

Charlie Taylor

"In these jails, prisoners continued to be locked in their cells for unacceptably long periods of time, with those who were not working or in education often only getting out for one or two hours a day. Prisoners frequently told me of the psychological effects of these long lock ups on a population with fragile mental health. Many were desperate to get into workshops or education, but insufficient staffing, combined with over-complicated and slow allocation processes, meant that they stayed stuck in their cells.

"We continued to be very concerned about the treatment of women who were displaying the most extreme mental health difficulties, particularly those who prolifically self-harmed. Many of them should not have been in prison and in most cases, the wait to transfer to hospital remained much too long. Prison officers and other staff do not have enough expertise to care for women with very complex needs and a huge amount of prison resource is taken up by a small number of cases. Given the lower risk that most women pose, there is no excuse for the poor outcomes in purposeful activity and a real drive from governors and the regional director is required to transform this situation."

And here is the most recent annual report and surprise, surprise, we find the same problems over and over again. Over-crowding, boredom, access to drugs, increased violence and lack of preparation for release. Here are just a few points from a long and detailed report.

"The annual report of HM Chief Inspector of Prisons from 1 April 2023 to 31 March 2024." (published 10 September 2024)

Charlie Taylor

"The increase in the prison population by 3,497 in the year to 31 March 2024 - a rise of 4% on the previous year - and the lack of available space is the dominating backdrop to this report, publication of which was delayed from July to September due to the General Election. Despite projections as far back as 2018 predicting this rise, successive governments have failed to build enough capacity to keep pace."

"Perhaps unsurprisingly, given the levels of overcrowding and shortage of experienced officers, key indicators of how safe our prisons are, such as the rates of assaults, self-harm and self-inflicted deaths, all remained high or increased over the past

year. The ingress of drugs either over the wall or through the gate were a common cause of violence, bullying and debt. Prisons are a lucrative market for organised crime gangs and restricting the supply through rigorous security measures was still not good enough in many jails."

"We judged safety to be poor or not sufficiently good at 11 of the 39 prisons and YOIs holding adult and young adult men and women."

"Many prisoners in these jails were trapped in a cycle of boredom, frustration and poor behaviour, which fuelled the demand for drugs and increased violence, debt and self-harm. This was often underpinned by poor relationships with staff, a failure to establish or reinforce the rules, and far too little purposeful activity."

"Violence was a priority concern in 14 adult male prisons we visited this year and was often a product of the illicit drug market."

"In 2023, there were 90 self-inflicted deaths in adult men's prisons, a rise of 27% from 2022, and three self-inflicted deaths in women's jails."

"We raised concerns about gaps in mental health provision at 12 sites this year. Most were about excessive waits for transfers to secure hospitals under the Mental Health Act, and the risks associated with delayed assessment and treatment while in prison."

"A lack of investment in ageing infrastructure and an inability to commission or undertake building work. Far too many buildings and systems needed upgrading, and the continued existence of night sanitation in some prisons was unacceptable."

"The effectiveness of education, skills and work activities in prisons was poor overall and had continued to decline, with prison leaders struggling to hold their education providers to *account where services were ineffective."*

"Jails often failed to fulfil their vital role in preparing prisoners coming to the end of their sentence for return to the community."

"Children's survey results cover the four YOIs and one STC inspected this year."

- *"We found drift and decline in conditions for children, despite substantial resources in the youth estate.*
- *There had been a breakdown of behaviour management and an overreliance on keeping children apart.*
- *There were poor relationships between staff and children.*
- *Children were not receiving the education to which they were entitled.*
- *Children's establishments were holding more young adults and children on remand."*

I think we can agree that the thoughtful and accurate reporting of the chief prison inspectors goes unheard by those who have any power to reform our prisons in any way, shape or form.

The silence is deafening. So many words, all to no avail.

And yet now, here are yet some more words about crime and justice which will be published in **April 2025**.

These will be from *The Times* newspaper which has established a **'Crime and Justice Commission'**, which it says is needed in the *"light of the knife crime crisis, shoplifting epidemic, growing threat of cybercrime, concerns about police culture, court backlogs, problems with legal aid, and overflowing prisons"*.

Two former Chief Inspectors of Prisons, who we have heard from many times, Peter Clarke and Nick Hardwick will join the *"high-powered panel which will consider the future of criminal justice and policing in the UK."*

It will hold fortnightly evidence sessions, with witnesses including police officers, victims, judges, lawyers, prison officers, scientists, business leaders and academics.

There will be five meetings of the whole commission over the course of the year.

They say that *"The commission will consult widely with victims and practitioners to identify problems in the system and work out pragmatic, practical solutions. The recommendations will be focused on the criminal justice system in England but the commission will also consider the lessons to be learnt from around the UK and examine international police, court and prison systems to identify examples of best practice."*

Hmm. Well having seen all the above I think we all know what is needed.

To start with I really hope they will consider lessons to be learnt throughout the Scandinavian countries. That would be good.

But here is some specific advice and indeed some criticism which I hope they might find helpful.

They are studying over ten different categories.

I will take each category in turn.

POLICING, INCLUDING THE CULTURE OF THE POLICE.

Well Baroness Casey of Blackstock is on the panel and she gave evidence at the very first session in April this year. Now she, you may remember, conducted a report into the culture and behaviour of the metropolitan police after the murder of Sarah Everard by a serving police officer. This report found widespread institutional failure saying that this police force was *"institutionally racist, misogynist and homophobic."* This report was published in March 2023. So she is very well qualified to state exactly what the problems are.

Obviously very many of our police are brave and dedicated professionals who do a dangerous and difficult job and at the other end of the spectrum Humberside Police was awarded one of the highest grades of any UK force following an inspection in **2022**. It received six *"outstanding"* grades and two *"good"* grades from His Majesty's Inspectorate of Constabulary and Fire and Rescue Services. So I am sure they will be able to identify 'best practice' from them.

KNIFE CRIME, GANGS AND ACQUISITIVE CRIME.

This is another area where action is urgently needed and where another panelist has experience. After the pandemic many youth services were unable to re-open which left a generation of vulnerable young people without life-changing support.

In 2021 almost two-thirds of youth organisations with incomes under £250,000 said they were at risk of closure. And former Children's Commissioner, Anne Longfield, who is sitting on the panel said that *"Areas suffering the most significant cuts in spending on young people have recorded larger increases in knife crime and drug-related crimes"*. She goes on to say *"Youth services are the last line of defence for vulnerable children. If these children have a bad time at home and don't have the structure of school, for whatever reason, and then you take away youth services too, they're completely on their own, with nothing protecting them from physical abuse, self-harm and drug use, being exploited and groomed."*

And here is the voice of a father who lost his son in a stabbing and who said that the closing down of youth centres across the country is *"pushing children to violence"*. Dwayne Roye, a community activist from Croydon, spoke to Sky News when he said he had *"hosted his* seventh annual football tournament today (22nd May 2022) to raise awareness about knife crime."

He manages Elite Development FC, a youth football team in Croydon, and he firmly believes budget cuts that have decimated youth services in parts of England - particularly south London - are linked to the rise in knife crime.

He told Sky News: "Every borough used to have a community centre - Brixton, Peckham, Croydon - but now they've all been shut down and this has had a terrible impact on our communities."

The Times Commission should look especially at two charities, The Youth Endowment Fund and the Ben Kinsella Trust.

'The Youth Endowment Fund' says "Our mission is to find what works to prevent children and young people from becoming involved in violence and to build a movement to put this knowledge into practice.

"To understand what works to prevent knife crime, we need to understand what drives a young person to pick up a knife in the first place. Our research covers a wide range of areas, from evaluating individual prevention projects to understanding the lives of young people."

'The Ben Kinsella Trust' says "We educate young people on the dangers of knife crime and help them to make positive choices to stay safe. Our workshops follow the journey of both the victim and the offender through a series of unique and immersive experiences to show young people how choices and consequences are intrinsically linked. "Our workshops change young people's attitudes to knife crime; debunking the myth that carrying a knife will protect you. They strengthen peer values; ensuring young people give better advice to each other and challenge peers who are carrying (or thinking of carrying) a knife". It was founded by the family of Ben Kinsella, who was stabbed to death in 2008, and runs workshops, exhibitions and campaigns to prevent knife crime.

I am sure they will be studying the brilliant work that these charities do, but I have to say that the new Labour government is already on it. They have just announced an amnesty on zombie knives and they have been added, together with machetes, to the list of illegal weapons. But I am absolutely amazed that this was not already the case.

VIOLENCE AGAINST WOMEN AND GIRLS.

This is another area which is in the news at the moment and is what some are calling an epidemic. And I have just discovered the most amazing charity called 'Centre for Women's Justice.' This charity was founded in 2016 and on its website it says *"We aim to bring together specialist lawyers, academics and other experts in the field of violence against women, with those working on the frontline as activists, survivors and service providers to bring strategic law challenges and ensure access to justice for victims of male violence."*

Their vision is for a society in which all state institutions work effectively to eradicate male violence against women and girls. Their mission is to hold the state to account and challenge discrimination in the justice system around male violence against women and girls. The following quote is highlighted. *"Violence against women continues to persist as one of the most heinous, systematic and prevalent human rights abuses in the world. It is a threat to all women, and an obstacle to all our efforts for development, peace, and gender equality in all societies. Violence against women is always a violation of human rights; it is always a crime; and it is always unacceptable. Let us take this issue with the deadly seriousness that it deserves."* — Ban Ki Moon, United Nations Secretary General

They support women by--

- *"Holding the state accountable for failures in the prevention of violence against women and girls.*
- *Supporting individuals and groups who challenge institutions and laws that perpetuate such violence.*

154

- *Undertaking strategic litigation and facilitating legal assistance.*
- *Bringing together victims, women's groups, lawyers, academics and other experts in the field of violence against women.*
- *Raising awareness of specific cases and issues arising from our work.*
- *Monitoring and challenging trends in policy, practice and the law which impacts on violence against women and girls."*

The complete website make inspirational reading.

But everyone must call this out. Every aspect of our society is culpable and needs to address this issue starting with education. From Reception to the Sixth form, for both boys and girls, there needs to be discussions, topics, projects, life stories and more, involving the word 'respect'.

But it needs immediate action in all work places, in sport, in culture, in the arts, in the police, in the NHS, in all aspects of the criminal justice system and in politics. We are hearing about too many violent crimes by men against women and girls just now and this needs to be addressed urgently.

And I am seeing that this is exactly what the new Labour government is doing. To be fair to the Times Commission, when this began in April 2024 a general election was still just being talked about and the likely date being bandied about was November. And after 14 years of inaction and incompetence from the Conservatives I can quite understand why they thought this Commission was a good idea.

But I can say that once again, after just 6 weeks in office, Labour are on the case. Keir Starmer is *"fired up"* by this issue and is setting up a separate board to focus on it. It will be chaired by Jess Phillips who was so vocal, when in opposition about, women and the appalling backlog of rape cases. She is now minster for safeguarding and violence against women and girls.

So.......police will be asked to use counter-terrorism style tactics to monitor 1.000 known most dangerous abusers. Domestic violence specialists will be introduced to 999 call centres. Police offices will not get promotion in future if they have had no experience in working in either a child protection or a domestic violence unit.

There will be a six month data-gathering exercise with input from the Home Office, education, health and other officials. So that will still be two months before the Times Commission is published as we have another eight months to wait for that.

CYBERCRIME, FRAUD AND ONLINE HARMS.

Well at last the Online Safety Bill has become law. This should make the internet safer for children.

This Bill which has taken years to become law puts the onus on firms to protect children from some legal but harmful material with the regulator Ofcom being given extra enforcement powers. It introduces new rules such as requiring pornography sites to stop children viewing content by checking ages. Platforms will also need to show they are committed to removing illegal content. Breaking the rules could result in fines of up to 10% of global revenue for tech companies, or £18m - whichever is bigger. Their bosses could also potentially face prison time as a punishment. However, platforms such as WhatsApp, Signal and iMessage say they cannot access or view anybody's messages without destroying existing privacy protections for all users, and have threatened to leave the UK rather than compromise message security. WhatsApp has definitely threatened to withdraw from the UK over the act. So they are not at all concerned about the safety of our children.

And many campaigners are saying it does not go far enough. Fact-checking organisation 'Full Fact', which supported the bill, said *"retrograde changes"* made to it meant it did not go far enough *"to address the way that platforms treat harmful misinformation and disinformation."* 'Full Fact's' head of policy and advocacy Glen Tarman continued: *"Our freedom of expression is left in the hands of self-interested internet companies, while dangerous health misinformation is allowed to spread rampant."*

So that needs a lot of tightening up.

THEN THERE IS FRAUD.

The National Audit Office revealed in March 2023 the staggering increase of money lost due to fraud since the pandemic hit compared to a couple of years before it. Over £7bn of the total relates to governmental schemes introduced during COVID. But a policy paper by the last government updated in June 2023 stated that *"This government will not tolerate the barrage of scam texts, phone calls, adverts, and emails that causes misery to millions and makes up over 40% of all crime."*

They are setting up a new National Fraud Squad (NFS) *"dedicated to pursuing the most sophisticated and harmful fraudsters, with over 400 new specialist investigators, and making tackling fraud a priority for police forces in England and Wales."*

So that needs checking out.

CYBERCRIME.

Several million cases of fraud and of computer misuse are reported to the police every year. It's staggering, but even more staggering is that so many of those crimes could have been prevented by making a few small changes in online behaviour. Basically this needs much more publicity and public awareness.

However I see that a 'Government Cyber Security Strategy' was set up in 2022 under the Johnson government which sets out how *"we will ensure that all government organisations - across the whole public sector - are resilient to the cyber threats we face." "To achieve its vision"* it goes on to say *"the strategy pursues a central aim - for government's critical functions to be significantly hardened to cyber-attack by 2025, with all government organisations across the whole public sector being resilient to known vulnerabilities and attack methods no later than 2030."* I think that one definitely needs checking out.

TERRORISM.

Here we have a review which came out in February 2023 under the Sunak government by the then Home Secretary Suella Braverman. It says that the *"Home Secretary has committed to delivering wholesale and rapid change across 'Prevent' following a major independent review into the programme."*

"The independent review recognises the need for 'Prevent' to better understand ideology and the individual agency of people who willingly support terrorism. The government's response will ensure that, in the face of an enduring terrorist threat to the UK, 'Prevent' can adequately address the dangerous ideologies which underpin it."

I am quite sure that the panel are absolutely on top of this one.

THE CAUSES OF CRIME (INCLUDING MENTAL HEALTH, SPECIAL EDUCATIONAL NEEDS AND ADDICTION)

I am presuming the panel will look far further than this. I believe they should also be looking at the cost of living crisis, absolute poverty, homelessness, coercive bullying, poor education, inadequate child-care, absentee parenting, lack of youth facilities, underfunded care homes for children and young people, unemployment and other environmental circumstances.

THE COURT SYSTEM.

Well they must all be *au fait* with what is happening in our criminal courts. They will know about the horrendous backlog, the shortage of barristers and judges, the problems locating prisoners, the crumbling and un-safe infrastructure and I will be very interested to see what plans they come up with.

SENTENCING POLICY AND THE JUDICIARY.

Well we have already seen that the sentencing policy is a complete minefield and so I am sure the panel have read the first annual lecture, in memory of Lord Ramsbotham, which was held on 29 November 2023. One of the speakers was Sir Bob Neill MP who was chair of the House of Commons Justice Committee. Now this Justice Select Committee had recently published a report, called **'Public Opinion and Understanding of Sentencing'** because, he said, *"we wanted to drive down into what are the drivers behind the sort of approach that politicians feel constrained to take towards penal policy and that showed there is a problem with the lack of a coherent approach to sentencing. Sentencing is done in a very ad hoc, very piecemeal way in this country in recent years. And in particular there's insufficient analysis of the potential effects on the prison population of what has been a ratchet in terms of increasing sentences.*

"For example, introducing the presumption of custodial sentences of less than 12 months should be suspended, I think that's a really important step forward, something that my committee recommended some time back. Alex's (Chalk) predecessor of course put it straight in the wastepaper basket, if I can put it that way. I'm delighted that wiser heads, that more enlightened heads are now in charge. Equally, we've then got to find robust alternatives that both sentencers – magistrates and judges – are confident in, that they will actually have an impact upon the individual, but also that the public is going to be confident in."

It really is worth reading the whole lecture as I am sure they will.

PRISONS, PROBATION AND REHABILITATION.

This is my book! I will send them a copy!

THE ROLE OF NEW TECHNOLOGY
AND FORENSICS.

Well on the 16th **July 2020** there was an evaluation of digital technology in prisons by the Ministry of Justice which said that *"In the last decade, Her Majesty's Prison and Probation Service has invested in installing technology widely in prisons in England and Wales. The technology has included: in-cell telephony, self-service kiosks and in-cell laptops, and mobile devices for prison staff. This report focuses on the impact of the technology on "the communication of knowledge within prisons, prisoner wellbeing and confidence using IT, prisoner relationships inside and outside prison, prison violence, and staff job satisfaction and workload."* So they were on it so far as new technology was concerned.

But then we hear of an enormous amount of wasted money on schemes that were not working. In December 2021 HM Prison and Probation Service spent £98.2m on a new Electronic Monitoring Programme used to monitor curfews and conditions of court or prison orders. But because it took so long to produce it was overtaken by more advanced technology and so it was scrapped.

Then the Courts and Tribunals Service spent a further £18 million on a digital case management system for court staff which has led to strike threats over its poor performance.

And in the days of Dominic Raab we heard that his department introduced new x-ray scanners in prisons to detect and prevent drugs, weapons and phones being smuggled in. The trouble was that according to an analysis of the MoJ figures by the Labour party they are only detecting a quarter the number of contraband items being found in manual checks by prison officers. They have spent £100 million on them so I think it needs checking out to see if they really do work now.

Technology does not appear to be a strong point at the moment although with a new government I do acknowledge that maybe things will change.

FORENSICS.

Well we have seen how crucial that is in crime cases for proving the innocence or guilt of someone.

In December 2022 there was an inspection by His Majesty's Inspectorate of Constabulary and Fire & Rescue Services into how well the police and other agencies use digital forensics in their investigations. This a part of what they said. *"It has become increasingly clear that the police service hasn't kept pace with the scale of the challenges they face. In some cases, we found that the police simply didn't understand what digital forensics meant. We found a national backlog of over 25,000 devices waiting to be examined. This didn't include all the devices likely to be in the system. "We found delays in some areas so egregious that victims were being failed. In some areas, the system of digital forensic examination is slow, ineffective and less professionally managed than the other police forensic disciplines. We also had little confidence that the police service had a coherent plan for improving the current situation"*. They made nine recommendations in this report and I am sure the panel will think it really important to check these out. '

So I will be interested to hear the conclusions of the Times Commission when they are published next April. But I am rather concerned when I hear that the meetings are held fortnightly and there are only five full face-to-face meetings in the year. I just do not feel any sense of urgency. There are some excellent people on the panel who are all experts in their fields, and I just wish they could work a bit faster. But I note that James Timpson resigned from the panel when he became prison's minister.

But as Sir Bob Neil said in the Ramsbotham lecture *"One of the frustrations I've had as chair of the Select Committee is that, with the justice system everybody nods along to it but they think nothing of it until they happen to have some direct connection themselves."*

Yes, I think we can all relate to that.

And now I hear that another existing scandal is escalating. Staffing of all prisons is in crisis. The Ministry of Justice said in 2023 that prison and probationary staffing levels in England and Wales were dangerously low.

As of **2024** around 15% of prisons are expected to have fewer than 80% of the required staff. So why is it that today, (**2nd August 2024**) the Ministry of Justice has decided to cut its funding to an amazing charity whose sole raison d'etre is to recruit and train brilliant graduates to become prison officers?

This is quite extraordinary. 'Unlocked Graduates' have had enormous successes. As they say on their website *"Our award-winning leadership development programme recruits outstanding graduates and career changers to become exceptional prison officers.*

"Unlocked Graduates was launched in 2016. Our programme has now been running for over eight years and we have placed over 750 officers in prisons across London, the South East, West Midlands, the North West and Wales."

They are devastated at the decision by the Ministry of Justice to abandon all of this.

They say that over the past eight years *"Unlocked has launched and run a hugely successful graduate leadership development programme for the prison service in England and Wales. Our participants have helped to transform the lives of tens of thousands of prisoners. We are therefore deeply saddened that we have been unable to agree terms with the Ministry of Justice to continue to deliver this work and, as a result, do not have a contract to recruit any further cohorts. This year, we were ranked 22nd in the Times Top 100 Best Graduate Employers list and had more than 40 applications per place. Prisons are, rightly, a national priority at the moment. This is a system facing real challenges. There has never been a greater need for innovative and excellent leaders to lead change from the inside out. Unlocked is a global leader in recruiting and training exactly these people to do exactly this. We hope in the coming weeks that the new government can work with Unlocked to find a way forward so we are able to recruit a 2025 cohort. Not doing so ultimately deprives the prison service of the talent it so desperately needs and deserves."* So, just one other task for our new government and we will listen out to hear if the new Secretary of State for Justice will see sense and work together with Unlocked Graduates and overturn this crazy decision.

It is quite extraordinary.

So I conclude with some wise words from Lady Susan Ramsbotham, wife of Sir David Ramsbotham, who left a note for her husband on the breakfast table to read shortly before he gave one of his final lectures before he retired as Chief Inspector of Prisons. This is what it said:-

> *"If prison worked, there would be work or education for every prisoner.*
>
> *If prison worked, we would be shutting prisons, not opening more.*
>
> *If prison worked, judges would not be seeing in the dock the same people, time over again.*

If prison worked, we would not be imprisoning more people than any other European country other than Turkey.

If prison worked, less children would be in care, less mothers would be in prison.

If prison worked, we would be saving billions of pounds with less prisons, less secure children's homes and fewer court cases."

I rest my case. Prison, in the UK, does not work.

But then, due to recent events, I really cannot conclude here.

SWIFT JUSTICE

For now, **August 2024**, the criminal justice system and our prisons are about to be overwhelmed when they are already overwhelmed. The far right racists do not appreciate a Labour government and so have used a knife attack on young girls on the 29th July to trigger riots in our streets. By accusing the attacker on Twitter and other social media of being an illegal immigrant, certain people have fuelled horrifying racial attacks in cities around the UK and we have been suffering daily riots for nearly two weeks. Libraries, a Citizen's Advice office, hotels with asylum seekers and hotels with nurses, have all been set on fire, and mosques and cars and cemeteries and gardens have all been vandalised.

The attacker was not an illegal asylum seeker and Nigel Farage MP, Elon Musk of Twitter, Lee Anderson MP, Robert Jenrick MP, Laurence Fox, Tommy Robinson amongst others, including the right wing media, are all guilty of spouting words which are an incitement to violence as with Elon Musk who said *"civil war will be inevitable."* There is a huge discussion on Twitter at the moment as to whether we should all leave or not. Some of us are saying that if the likes of us leave we just give it up to the racists and the Starmer bashers so we are staying on and refusing to call it X.

But the mis-information is appalling. Actually I say *"mis-information"* but as someone was saying to the BBC that is just a euphemism for telling lies. These people are liars and that is what they should be called. Sir Keir Starmer is well aware of the trap these people are trying to set up for him. They are all shouting *"bring in the army"* but he is responding in the way he knows best which is through the courts of law. So many of these attacks were caught on video because they were all, excitedly and rather stupidly, filming others and even themselves so facial recognition technology will be able to catch those responsible. Courts are sitting 24 hours 7 days a week and already (7th August) there have been over 400 arrests and many given prison sentences.

Starmer says they will all face the full force of the law.

But of course, as you will understand if you have read this book our prisons are full and the backlog of cases is at an all- time high.

The Law Society of England and Wales president Nick Emmerson said *"We deplore the violent scenes and rioting that we have witnessed across the past week."* He goes on to say that *"It is paramount that justice is done for all those who have been involved in, or are victims of, the riots. We commend the UK government for its swift response and want to see that the necessary support and resources are provided for both prosecution and defence lawyers, courts staff and judiciary in dealing with this emergency. The criminal justice system has suffered significant neglect over the last decade and has less resilience and flexibility with severe backlogs in the magistrates' and Crown courts."*

He goes on to say that *"The criminal defence profession is also depleted and over-worked and the goodwill of the solicitors who are being called on to work additional antisocial hours is fast running out."*

Then of course our prisons are full. However the government has said that it would make more than 567 new prison places available including extra cells at HMP Stocken, Rutland, and Cookham Wood. Cookham Wood if you remember was closed down as a YOI in March this year and re-opened as a male adult prison so I think there will still be some room there.

But Carl Davies, vice-president of the Prison Governors' Association has warned that the justice system was *"still reeling from the impact of austerity"*, adding that: *"To think we can already turn on the system to respond in the same way we did to the 2011 riots is probably a bit unrealistic."*

Well yes. We have seen how successive governments have completely destroyed our criminal justice system so this all comes at a really critical time. Keir Starmer has hardly had time to get his feet under the table at Downing Street but as a former prosecuting lawyer is the best person to sort it out.

And now 'Operation Early Dawn' has been re-introduced. (19th August 2024). This was last actioned in May (2024) by the Conservatives. It means that offenders, when arrested, will be held in police cells until a prison place can be found. So it is all over the news that our prisons are full and our courts are jammed and people are calling for long-term solutions. Absolutely and exactly what John Howard was calling for in 1777.

Were these riots pre-planned as soon as they realised that Labour was on course to win the election? Did the Conservative government deliberately weaponise asylum seekers and vilify them in order to stoke up resentment and hate amongst the right-wing members of the population? Did they deliberately destroy the criminal justice system so that it would be difficult to control this situation?

Well these are questions being asked by many at the moment.

The police are saying that they hope to be *"through the worst"* of the disorder but are ready to respond if the situation escalates. 6,000 riot officers around the country are braced to intervene as and when necessary and the Met say that 1,300 public order officers are ready to be deployed across the capital.

There are over 100 more riots planned for this weekend (9th August 2024) and there was a list of places and times on Twitter so the police know exactly where to go. It is all looking very worrying and people are being warned to stay inside. So we will see what happens.

Well what happened was the most amazing and uplifting situation you could possibly imagine.

"I speak for the British people" is what Suella Braverman used to say as Home Secretary when defending her Rwanda deportation scheme and demonising asylum seekers.

Well the British people stood up and spoke for themselves last night to her and to all racists and completely trashed them all. Not with bricks and stones or fire bombs or offensive language but with dignity, decency, strength, wonderful wit, kindness and love.

We looked on in amazement as we saw thousands of people taking to the streets of cities up and down the country, not in anger, but with a calm and determined dignity, showing the rioters how unrepresentative they were of the British population.

We saw them in Newcastle, Liverpool, Birmingham, Walthamstow, Bristol, Sheffield, Middlesborough, Oxford, Cambridge, Southampton, London, Brighton and others. You literally could not see the roads for people. The rioters were completely blocked out.

Oh no wait a minute. They managed to occupy a roundabout in Blackpool for a few minutes. *"We want our island back"* they were chanting but I never thought that this was what they meant. And the response from Brighton was brilliant. As the rioters arrived by train they were greeted with drag-queens and a samba band. As someone said who on earth would think it was a good idea to take right-wing ideology to a place like Brighton? The chant went up:-

"We are many, you are few. We are Brighton, who are you?"

Then in every city we saw the placards saying *"Refugees welcome"* and *"Say it loud and say it clear. Refugees are welcome here."* *"Love not hate". "Your racism is not our patriotism".* But, as we had seen Nazi salutes, I think my favourite is the one which read *"Nans against Nazis"* held up by a pensioner who was defending a mosque in Liverpool. And whilst watching this brave and intrepid woman we saw an elderly gentleman leaning on his stick and playing the Beatles number 'Give peace a chance' on his phone.

Oh my word, we watched all this on Twitter and a little of it on television and simply couldn't believe our eyes. Even a BBC presenter was amazed and actually sounded a bit disappointed as the cameras rolled down a street full of police vans as he was saying *"well we thought there might be some rioters down here but we can't seem to find any."*

Here are the true people of Britain; the same people who appeared after the riots to clear up the devastation and to offer food and drink to the exhausted and battered police. The publishers who are giving books to the library which was torched and who say they will make it even better than it was before.

And the swift justice goes on. Our over-stretched criminal justice system is responding to this emergency in brilliant fashion.

Yvette Cooper, Home Secretary said that police forces have been backed by government to take the *"strongest possible action against every level of perpetrator"*, while the number of prosecuting lawyers on call have been increased and the Director of Public Prosecutions Stephen Parkinson promised *"severe consequences"* and said CPS prosecutors are working *"around the clock"* to bring cases to court.

Well already there have been trials and convictions and some are already in prison.

Those inciting violence on social media are also under threat and the CPS is likely to be looking at possible offences under the Public Order Act 1986, including incitement to commit an offence including rioting. Indeed, speaking to BBC Breakfast on Monday, Ms. Cooper said: *"Social media companies need to take some responsibility, we also need to make sure that criminal activity online is being pursued."*

And already a woman in Northampton remains in custody after being arrested on suspicion of inciting racial hatred on social media and a face-book user who urged people to attack a Leeds hotel housing asylum seekers has been sent to prison.

The police are saying they know who you are so just wait for the knock on the door or, I would imagine, the dawn raid.

And they really do need to know the penalties involved.

The offence of violent disorder carries a maximum penalty of five years in prison, with the toughest penalties reserved for those who are armed, use petrol bombs, lead the violence, and target people in a mob attack. If someone is charged with rioting, the maximum penalty is ten years in prison. Looters will face a burglary charge with a maximum penalty of 14 years in prison.

Prosecutors will also be considering arson charges for those responsible for the fires last week. Arson carries a maximum penalty of life imprisonment.

So who are these rioters exactly? Well Lee Anderson MP, said: *"I'm sure there's a lot of young lads out there, the British working class lads, you know, throwing stones and damaging things, they're not far-right thugs."* He said that *"we all do daft things when we're young."*

Really Mr. Anderson? Did you completely trash buildings, set fire to hotels, grab bricks from garden walls and raid cemeteries to pull up grave stones to throw at the police and attack Muslims and mosques? No these are mostly criminals many already known to the police and they **are** racists and they **are** right-wing thugs.

By the 10th August there had been 741 arrests and 302 people have been charged. These figures are expected to rise over the coming weekend. (And indeed they did. By the 12th August, there had been 900 arrests and 466 charges.)

And as I say they were all filming the criminal things that they were doing. It is all on camera. Their faces are all over Twitter as the police ask people to help identify them. In fact one even had his name printed on the back of his t-shirt so that was a bit of a clue.

The one I remember most is of a man and woman pushing a smoking wheelie-bin, which they had set on fire, towards a line of police. The man ran off but the woman kept pushing the bin which went faster and faster until she fell flat on her face at the feet of the police. I think she will be a bit more careful in future when she puts the bins out. She is already in prison.

Starmer is doing really well and all over Twitter he is being called 'Top Tier Keir'.

He has, of course cancelled his holiday, whilst the leader of the opposition whose name, in case you have forgotten is Rishi Sunak, is on a five week break in Beverly Hills.

So how did we get here? Where has the racist element of our society come from?

I think we need to look to our politicians, to the language they have used and to the actions they have taken. We go back to the referendum in 2016 when David Cameron gave in to his right-wing cabal and he called for the referendum to decide on whether or not we should leave the European Union. So the word Brexit entered the English language to their ever-lasting shame. It was the most disastrous, self-inflicted catastrophe ever inflicted on the British people. The fact that, by a tiny majority people voted in favour of it, merely proves that the leave campaign was a pack of lies helped, some believe, by Russian influences. Today nearly 60% would vote to re-join.

But the language of people such as Boris Johnson, Priti Patel, Suella Braverman, Dominic Raab and others has been disgraceful. The attack on lawyers has been ignorant and abusive. Any time we hear that lawyers have defeated the government's desires to deport asylum seekers we hear about *"leftie lawyers" "politically motivated lawyers"*, lawyers *"abetting the work of criminal gangs"*, and European judges accused of being *"racists"*. Refugees have been demonised and we hear about an *"invasion on our southern coast."*

George Monbiot, journalist in the Guardian wrote on the 6th August 2024 *"For 14 years, the Conservatives and their friends in the media whipped up racism and Islamophobia. These riots are the result."*

It is a long article so I just pick out two examples. He goes on to say *"When Suella Braverman, the former home secretary, falsely claimed that Britain was "sleepwalking into a ghettoised society", and that "Islamists ... are in charge now"*, she was allowed by Rishi Sunak to stay on the party benches." And then he says, *"Robert Jenrick, now a contender for the Tory leadership, claimed in parliament, without evidence: "We have allowed our streets to be dominated by Islamist extremists."*

Those are such appalling things to say **from our own government.**

And our media has also been irresponsible in the extreme. We expect it from the Mail and the Telegraph but even the BBC has been complicit. The amount of air time that they have given to Nigel Farage is disgraceful. He was given space on the television programme 'Question Time' more than anyone else bar one, so building him up to become a major public figure forever spouting rubbish.

Actually he has gone a bit quiet at the moment and no one has seen him anywhere. His constituents in Clacton are writing to him and phoning Reform UK but to no avail. No-one knows where he is. It could have something be to do with the fact that 'Farage Riots' is trending on Twitter I suppose. He is probably back in his home in Brussels.

But of course one person who can never be quiet is our ex- MP and ex- PM Boris Johnson. He is more than happy to continue to stoke up division and hate.

Writing in the Daily Mail his headline reads *"BORIS JOHNSON: Time to pack the Factor 50, Keir, check out of Britain - and reflect on the frenzy of utter stupidity Labour's embarked on."* He continues *"nothing excuses a government that seems deaf to public concerns, and that suggests, moreover, that they actively dislike all members of the public who share those concerns."*

You see? Some people never learn from their stupidity.

Sir Keir cancelled his holiday as you would expect of a serious prime minister in difficult times unlike Johnson of course who will never miss a holiday.

Why does he think anyone is remotely interested in what he has to say?

Then there are others who are accusing the police of 'Two tier policing'. This ignorant and disgusting myth has prompted attacks on officers across the country often resulting in serious injury. They are implying that white working-class Britons are policed more harshly than ethnic minorities. They compare the policing of the Palestinian marches with the policing of the rioters. The commissioner of the Metropolitan Police called this theory *"complete nonsense"*.

Do we have to explain this very carefully? It would appear so. On the Palestinian marches no-one broke the law. They didn't set fire to hotels, torch libraries, hurl bricks at the police etc. The rioters **did** break the law. They tried to kill people. South Yorkshire's Metro Mayor spoke about the violence in Rotherham. He said that seasoned police officers were shocked at the scale of violence. The mob who stormed the hotel in Manvers were not attacking the hotel he said, they were attacking the people in the hotel. They were attacking the community. He said *"They were trying to*

hurt people. They were absolutely trying to hurt people." He went on
to say that the only thing that stopped them was the bravery of
the police officers who were "*some of the most brave and dedicated
people I've ever seen.*" Well I hope that has cleared that up.

And there is one other thing I would like to clear up too. In an
article in The Sunday Times today by Gabriel Pogrund and Harry
Yorke they say that Keir Starmer is an unpopular prime minister
and some are calling him 'Two tier Keir' as they are questioning the
different sentences being handed out. Well I have news for them.
They might have been looking at a YouGove poll but where I am
on Twitter 'Top Tier Keir' is trending and people are saying very
positive things about him. I see phrases such as "*No histrionics, or
sound bites, cool and dignified*". "*At last*" they say "*a PM who behaves
like a PM, proud of my prime minister, the first proper PM since Gordon
Brown, a damn good job, no drama Starmer, top-tier keir. He's really
doing an excellent job*".

But what is happening now? It is Saturday the 10th of August and
we see a huge tidal wave of goodness, decency, intelligence and
hope, sweeping the country. Actually it is more like a tsunami.
We hear the initials SUTR from an articulate, fine young man
who is standing outside the Reform UK offices in London together
with about 2,000 others. By the time they had walked to Trafalgar
Square it had grown to 5,000.

So what does SUTR stand for? It is 'Stand Up To Racism'. And my
word what a powerful organisation it is. There was no sign of any
rioters anywhere.

In Hull there were 400 anti-racists chanting "*When immigration
rights are under attack, what do we do, unite, push back.*" 3,000 people
joined an anti-racist rally in Glasgow. Two fascists turned up but
were chased away by the crowd and the police had to rescue them.
Over 2,000 anti-racists turned out in Edinburgh, 450 in Dundee,
500 in Norwich, 300 in Cambridge, 200 in Southend and 300 in
Wakefield near Leeds. Shrewsbury reported 'SUTR 500, fascists 20'

who soon decided to leave. Further rallies were held in Leicester, Oxford, Portsmouth, Hastings, Chesterfield, Manchester, Finsbury Park Mosque, Coventry, Liverpool, Newcastle, Harlow, Nottingham, Birmingham, Hackney, and Brixton. And in Belfast there were crowds of 15,000 who chanted 'When migrants' rights are under attack, what do we do? Stand up, fight back'.

'Rock Against Racism' concerts are returning in cities and towns recently affected by the anti-immigration riots. The first concert will be in London in September. 'Love Music Hate Racism' began in 2002 in response to the rise of the British National Party.

So to be clear: - The vast and over-whelming majority of the British public are welcoming to refugees. There is no such thing as two-tier policing or two-tier Keir. But there is a definite feel-good factor in the UK just now and it is largely due to 'Top Tier Keir'.

Yes, as we have seen, there are many causes for those riots apart from rampant racism, including lack of levelling up and extreme despair in many run-down towns and cities, but I do believe that there is hope for the future at last. But it will not be a quick fix.

IN CONCLUSION

I end up, where I began, in our prisons.

Our new Justice Secretary, Shabana Mahmood, has just said the riots would set back Labour's plans to fix the system, already struggling with a huge backlog of court cases and overcrowding in prisons. She said that the impact of the appalling scenes on the country's streets will be felt in the criminal justice system *"for months and years."*

Whilst I can understand her thinking, actually I have to disagree. I really do not like having to criticise our new Labour Justice Secretary but I think it will make no difference whatsoever. It should actually put a rocket under people involved which would be excellent.

We have seen how the judiciary can act quickly in an emergency. Of course it will take years to remedy all that needs to be remedied but with the will, the skill, the funding, the hard work, the coming together it can be done and it should, actually, have already begun. We all know the prisons have been over-crowded for years but they have found extra places for the rioters as they are already releasing some prisoners early. Get some education and therapy and anger management into the prisons at top speed so that these 'thugs' come out better people than when they went in. All that has happened in the last few weeks will not make things worse. It should galvanise you all into action.

ACTION is what is needed. Please no more words, no more excuses, no more reports, no more blame, no more wringing of hands. Yes I know you have only been in the job for about six weeks Justice Secretary and I am being a bit harsh maybe, but this is your beginning, this is your chance to make a difference. Please don't view these last dreadful weeks as a set-back and a massive headache, view them as an opportunity. You have a brilliant prisons minister in James Timpson and a brilliant ex-head of the CPS as your boss in Sir Keir Starmer. You **can** make a difference. So I go back to my very first sentence in this book. Please keep more women out of prison and make it illegal to put pregnant women in jail.

Eleven countries (with a total population of about 646 million) prohibit the imprisonment of pregnant women, or severely curtail it. They include the Russian Federation, Ukraine, Georgia, Brazil, Mexico and Colombia. Instead of prison they use house arrest, electronic monitoring or probation supervision. Portugal and Italy also have laws which protect pregnant women from being sent to prison. We can learn from these countries. To respect and protect the unborn child should be an important element in the criminal justice system of any civilised society.

I know that new sentencing guidelines came into force on April 1st 2024 but although it would appear that there are more mitigating factors for pregnant women I don't believe we are yet on a par with countries such as Russia or Colombia who, as I say, ban the imprisonment of all pregnant women.

I say again, that whilst this particular practice is inhumane, it is also a fact that for the vast majority of people in custody, in the UK, prison has not 'worked' and will not 'work.' For as we have seen, most of the ways in which all people are treated in our prisons is inhumane. Women's prisons, young offenders and adult male prisons are all in need of a radical overhaul.

Just today (20th August), we hear of a male prisoner being *"kettled."*

Do you know what that is? It is when boiling water is thrown over someone causing severe burns and injuries. Well a 31 year old prisoner decided it was a good idea to attack another inmate using this method which is shocking. By rights he should have been moved from his cell on to another landing after this. He wasn't and so four other inmates stormed into his cell just the day before he was due to be released and *"kettled"* him in revenge. They then beat him *"to a pulp"* and we hear from a source inside the prison that *"One lad kicked him in the head on the way out and broke his neck."*

So the murders continue.

The prison which enabled this behaviour is the newest prison in the UK called HMP Fosse Way. It is a category C private prison run by Serco. On its web site it states that it provides a *"secure, safe and decent environment."*

I go back to the quote by Dostoevsky who said that *"The degree of civilisation in a society can be judged by entering its prisons."*

I will leave you to draw your own conclusions.

This new government has its work cut out to restore so much that is broken in Britain today. The NHS, education, homelessness, children in poverty, youth clubs and more and I have written about them all in my previous books. But a just and adequately funded criminal justice system is essential to a well-ordered, functioning society.

By all means build some new smaller and more local prisons but demolish the Victorian relics which are still standing today and at the same time vastly reduce the prison population.

But, please, we do not need any more reports telling us how bad things are and what needs to be done.

WE KNOW.

GLOSSARY

HMP	His Majesty's Prison
HMPPS	His Majesty's Prison and Probation Service
YOI	Young Offenders Institution
HMIP	His Majesty's Inspectorate of Prisons
YCS	Youth Custody Service
SIDS	Sudden Infant Death Syndrome
CPIA	Criminal Procedure and Investigations Act
CCRC	Criminal Cases Review Commission
HMPPS	His Majesty's Prison and Probation Service
PSR	Pre-Sentence Report
NAO	National Audit Office
HMCTS	His Majesty's Courts and Tribunal Service
IPP	Imprisonment for Public Protection
VHCC	Very High Cost (Criminal) Cases
PPS	Public Prosecution Service
LASPO	Legal Aid Sentencing and Punishment of Offenders
CTI	Critical Time Intervention
CHAS	Children Heard and Seen
RASSO	Rape and Serious Sexual Abuse Cases
NFS	National Fraud Squad
CPS	Crown Prosecution Service
SUTR	Stand Up To Racism

ACKNOWLEDGEMENTS

BIBLIOGRAPHY

'Just Law' by Helena Kennedy

'Against All Odds' by Angela Cannings

'The Secret Barrister' by The Secret Barrister

'Fake Law' by The Secret Barrister

'Prisongate' by Lord David Ramsbotham

'Invisible' Women by Angela Devlin

My thanks go to all the charities involved in prison reform and to all the journalists who endeavour to keep this in the main stream media.

ABOUT THE AUTHOR

Sue Wood was born and brought up in a medical family in Coventry. She was educated in Leamington Spa and Maria Grey Froebel College in Twickenham. She worked as a Primary school teacher in Coventry and Cambridge and then took a break from teaching and worked as Director of Public Relations at Coventry Cathedral. After her wedding there she moved with her husband first to Abu Dhabi and then to Aberdeen. She is now settled in Hertfordshire with her husband and has two children and two grand-children.

She returned to teaching, first in Bushey and then in Elstree. On retiring she became a volunteer Speaker for Save the Children. She has been member of the Howard League for Penal Reform for over 30 years.

She started writing at the age of 10 when her American aunt gave her a 5 year diary, and she has written many books for family and friends. Her first four published books for the general public are:-

- **Beneath the Bluster.** A Diary of Despair. Ignorance, Incompetence, Confusion and Lies. The Conservative Government 2019-2021
- **Behind the Headlines.** A Parallel Universe. Arrogance, Corruption, Dither and Delay. The Conservative Government 2021-2022.
- **Britain Betrayed.** Slash and Burn. Delusional, Dysfunctional, Dishonest, and Degenerate. The Conservative Government 2022-2023.
- **Our Lost Children.** Silent voices. Damaged lives.

She has always been interested in news and politics, and these four books record exactly how it was possible for the far right to explode on our streets in 2024.

Made in the USA
Las Vegas, NV
07 February 2025

17666375R00105